Praise for ~~Presentation~~
to Standing Ovation

"This book is full of valuable ideas and techniques for how to become a great speaker. I highly recommend it."
–Jack Canfield, Coauthor of *The Success Principles* and the *Chicken Soup for the Soul* series

"This extraordinary book is loaded with great ideas you can use immediately to be a more powerful and persuasive speaker."
–Brian Tracy, CPAE Hall of Fame Speaker, has given 5000 speeches in 75 countries

"I'm glad Ron wrote this book because I'm a firm believer that the wisest investment is wisdom, and this book is full of wisdom."
–Jayson Gaignard, Founder, MastermindTalks

"If you need to quickly gain more confidence in captivating your audience every time you speak then this book will really help!"
–Mark Bowden, TRUTHPLANE® Presentation Training

"Ron's book is a powerful read that got me even more excited about the tremendous impact a presentation can make."

–Shawn Mintz, President, MentorCity

"You somehow managed to turn an encyclopedia of information about public speaking into a readable and memorable book with practical suggestions. Well done."

–Blake Kurisko, Partner, Miller Thompson LLP

"It's an easy read, I read it over a weekend. Its small size belies the number of valuable lessons contained within, yet it's very succinct! I will re-read every time I prepare a speech!"

–Kendra Shimmin, Manager, Membership Services, Insurance Brokers Association of Canada

"This book offers sage advice for packing class, elegance, power and punch into any presentation, and may well save serious speakers time, effort and embarrassment. And the bonus? This volume contains numerous interpersonal communication suggestions that are transferable to private life, too!"

–Nina Spencer, Keynote Speaker, Presentations Coach, and Author of *Getting Passion Out of Your Profession*

"Clear. Clever. Classy and Current. Ron Tsang gets my standing ovation. He has totally nailed it. My advice. Buy two copies and keep one locked up: this book has legs."

–Nicholas Boothman, Author of *How to Make People Like You in 90 Seconds or Less*

"You want a shortcut to becoming a powerful and profitable speaker? Buy, read, and apply Ron's book!"
–Tom Stoyan, Canada's Sales Coach,
HoF (Hall of Fame Speaker)

"Ron has written a powerful tool for people to guide them to the highest level of presentations. Whether internal to small groups or external to thousands, the practical and philosophical information in this book is truly priceless!"
–Alvin Law, CSP (Certified Speaking Professional),
HoF (Hall of Fame Speaker)

"Ron Tsang has written THE definitive book on presenting with power, influence, and poise. From the basic building blocks all the way to advanced techniques used by professional speakers, successful political candidates, and seasoned corporate leaders, it's all in here in one clearly-laid out package. Nothing is assumed and nothing is left out. If you want a book to take you from zero to hero in your presentation prowess, this book is it. Buy a copy for everyone on your team. Yes, it's that good."
–David Newman, CSP (Certified Speaking Professional) and Author of *Do It! Marketing*

"A lot of authors have written books on public speaking. Some of them I never finished. I read [From Presentation to Standing Ovation] from start to finish. It was fun, I got some good ideas, and I think you will too."
–Kaye Parker, *The Chronicle Herald*

Free Resources

For free companion tools and downloads, visit
rhtsang.com/book

RON TSANG

FROM PRESENTATION
TO STANDING
OVATION

Bulk discounts available.
For details please call (647) 885-0227
or email: info@rhtsang.com

Copyright © 2016-2017 Ron Tsang.

Printed in the United States of America.

ISBN: 9781517455989

This book is dedicated to my parents.

Contents

Introduction

You can have brilliant ideas,
but if you can't get them across,
your ideas won't get anywhere.

- LEE IACOCCA

Your message is more important than you know.

It was the summer of 1979. First-time parents Francis and Hasul had recently moved from New York. And they were preparing to celebrate Francis' birthday. But their adorable one-year-old baby boy was crankier than usual.

Francis and Hasul discovered that their baby had developed a dangerous, high fever: 103 degrees Fahrenheit, or 40 degrees Celsius. They said: "We need to see a doctor right away!"

At one of the best hospitals in the city, their doctor said: "Persistent high fever. Swollen lymph nodes. Could he have meningitis?"

The doctor ordered:

"Give him an IV!"
"Give him a chest x-ray!"
"Give him a spinal tap!"

But the lab results were inconclusive. The antibiotic treatments were ineffective. And the baby's fever raged for another three days.

The doctor had never seen this condition before. He noted, "Continuous high fever. Enlarged lymph glands. But no other symptoms?" The doctor didn't know what to do. How do you think Francis and Hasul must have felt?

Hasul never left her baby's side. For days, she slept overnight on a hospital room chair. And after finishing work each night, Francis reunited with his wife and child. Sometimes he slept in the car. But Francis and Hasul were resilient. They prayed every day that their family would have a better tomorrow.

After two weeks, the child's fever broke. Francis and Hasul noticed several new symptoms. The skin on their baby's fingers and toes began to peel off, like a glove. Inside the child's nose and throat were deformed mucous membranes. And his lips and tongue were as red as a strawberry.

The doctor said, "Why does that seem familiar?"

The doctor had just returned from a medical conference. He remembered hearing a speaker at the conference introduce a mysterious new pediatric disorder called *Kawasaki Disease*.

Your message is more important than you know.

The doctor glanced at his notes and said to Francis and Hasul: "We know what's wrong with your baby: he has Kawasaki Disease."

"But Kawasaki Disease causes lethal systemic inflammation. Your baby could die from a heart attack!"

The doctor added: "The only treatment is aspirin. A lot of aspirin—12 baby aspirins a day."

So Francis and Hasul took their baby back home. For the next six months they gave the boy 12 baby aspirins a day. And he survived!

Francis and Hasul were my parents, and I was the baby. I was Canada's first known survivor of Kawasaki Disease!

Why did I survive? Because my parents didn't give up on me. Because doctors don't keep their knowledge to themselves—they give it to others. Because I was meant to share this message with you.

Over 30 years ago, someone spoke at a conference. They shared their observations, experience, and expertise—and it saved my life!

A speaker saved my life.

Your words, your voice, and your actions give you the ability to improve the lives of those around you. And you never know who needs to listen to exactly what you have to say.

Your message is more important than you know!

Invest in yourself

If you're a business owner, expert, or influencer, your speaking skills must be an asset, not a liability. The best person to articulate your vision is you. Giving a successful sales, investor, or conference presentation will grow your business, promote your brand, and increase your impact. According to peak performance coach Tony Robbins, "The way we communicate with others and with ourselves ultimately determines the quality of our lives."

If you're an employee or a student, you may have the desire to climb the organizational ladder. But how will you know which skills will be the most in-demand in the future? As Harvard professor William H. Bossert notes, "If you're afraid that you might be replaced by a computer, then you probably can be—and should be."

Research firm Oxford Economics asked employers which skills they'll need the most in the next five to ten years. They discovered that the top priorities include strong interpersonal and communication skills.

These include vital skills such as relationship building, teamwork, and co-creativity. The trend is an increasing demand for high quality personal interaction.[1]

Performing well at work is becoming less about what you know and more about how we interact with others. Whether you're having a conversation with one person, or with a thousand, all speaking is public speaking!

How this book is organized

This book is divided into three parts:

Part One: Gain Unstoppable Confidence
Part Two: Deliver Unforgettable Messages
Part Three: Create Unbreakable Connections

Part One is all about your attitude. Do you have the confidence to speak in front of any audience? If you're an experienced speaker who doesn't have a problem with confidence, you might benefit most from reading **Part Two: Deliver Unforgettable Messages** and **Part Three: Create Unbreakable Connections**. Later on, you can come back to all the fun you missed in Part One.

Part Two will help you craft your presentation outline. You'll organize and optimize your thoughts by filling out the following template: **The Ovation Outline for Speeches™**. Are you wondering how to memorize your talk? In the last chapter of Part Two, you'll learn how to speak without notes.

---

[1] Read the survey at http://j.mp/talent2021

Part Three will reveal how you can become a more engaging presenter. Do you want to tell intriguing stories, make audiences laugh, and speak with powerful language? Do you want to be compelling, interactive, to speak with vocal variety, and have more persuasive body language? If so, this section is a must-read.

How to get the most from this book

As philosopher Ralph Waldo Emerson observed, "All the great speakers were bad speakers at first." And one of the fastest ways to succeed at something is to learn from people who are already successful in doing that thing—in this case, speaking.

Sometimes the quickest way to improve is to learn from your **opposite speaking personality type.**

Are you outgoing, emotional, and people-oriented like television host Ellen Degeneres or rock star Bono? If so, improve your presentations by using a framework to structure your thoughts. To see what I mean, make sure you read **Part Two: Deliver Unforgettable Messages**.

Are you an outgoing, task-oriented, Type A personality like Judge Judy or Ari Gold, the character from TV's *Entourage?* You can avoid alienating important people by building more empathy with your audience. Cut to the chase and be sure to read **Chapter 2: Flip Your Focus**.

Are you reserved, analytical and detail-oriented, like Facebook founder Mark Zuckerberg or Mr. Spock, the character from TV's *Star Trek*? Amplify your impact by setting a course, maximum warp, for **Part Three: Create Unbreakable Connections**.

Are you a more reserved, humble, people-oriented person, like Diana, Princess of Wales, or former U.S. President Jimmy Carter? You might find it helpful to read **Part One: Gain Unstoppable Confidence**.

Get started now

I hope that this jumping-off point will get you started, and help you get the most out of this book. Of course, invest the extra time in yourself to read it from cover to cover, and you'll benefit even more!

As the Chinese proverb says, "The best time to plant a tree is twenty years ago. The second best time is now." If you're scheduled to give a presentation in the future, please don't put it off. Hone your skills, and prepare today.

You're already off to a great start. Read on, and apply what you learn to your speaking. Then begin achieving all the results you desire!

Set your goals high, and don't stop till you get there.

- BO JACKSON

Part One: Gain Unstoppable Confidence

Chapter 1
Lose Your Anxiety

Champions aren't made in the gyms. Champions are made from something they have deep inside them: a desire, a dream, a vision.

- MUHAMMAD ALI

If you had the opportunity to meet one of the richest people in the world, what would *you* ask them?

During an MBA class trip to Omaha, Nebraska, I had the pleasure of meeting Warren Buffett. The Oracle of Omaha was very energetic and jovial. His dark suit and thick tortoise-shell glasses contrasted with his tousled white hair.

I asked him if he had a *granddaughter.*

Just kidding. But my favorite question was, "What was your best investment?"

Without blinking an eye, Warren Buffett said: "My best investment—was investing in myself!"

Throughout the first two decades of his life, Warren Buffett feared public speaking. He would throw up whenever he thought about getting up in front of a room to speak. But that all changed when he committed to improving his condition.

The best investment Warren Buffett ever made was developing his communication and persuasion skills. He attended two prestigious Ivy League universities: Wharton and Columbia. But he doesn't hang up those degrees on his wall. The only certificate he displays is from his course on public speaking.

Since then, Warren Buffett has spoken eloquently around the world. At the Berkshire Hathaway annual general meetings, 40,000 people hang onto his every word. The audience is large enough to fill an entire football stadium.

Warren Buffett's best investment was in himself. He went from not wanting to speak to not wanting to stop.

What are you doing to invest in yourself? How are you honing your communication and persuasion skills? How are you getting more of the results you desire when you speak?

You and I may not be Warren Buffett, but since you've read this far, you're on the right track!

Feel the fear and do it anyway

On a scale of 1 to 10, how would you rate your own confidence in public speaking?

According to popular surveys, public speaking is one of the things we fear more than death. Most people do experience some degree of anxiety when speaking in front of a group of people.

Public speaking anxiety is a prehistoric defense mechanism. Psychologists believe that we aren't nervous because we feel embarrassed or judged, but because we fear rejection. Back then, if early humans were cast out from the tribe, they would have to defend themselves all alone against predators. Complete rejection would most likely be a death sentence.

But in today's world, unless we have the courage to take risks, we place serious limits on what we can do. As personal fulfillment expert Jack Canfield says, "Everything you want is on the other side of fear."

What's the most popular remedy for public speaking nervousness? You may hear this a lot: "Just picture the audience naked." Or, "Just be yourself." Or, "Just try to stay calm." But if you're giving an important presentation, you deserve better advice!

Do you want to develop unstoppable speaking confidence? As author Dan Millman notes, "You don't have to control your thoughts. You just have to stop letting them control you." And you can start by not bottling up your anxiety.

Recent research shows that you'll have an easier time if you acknowledge your fear and reframe it as excitement.[2] Instead of thinking: "I'm too scared to speak," tell yourself: "I can't wait to speak." Instead of seeing a dangerous situation, you'll see an opportunity. Pivot your panic into excitement and you'll feel more confident.

Professional athletes and elite performers have learned how to "turn on," get focused, and build confidence in their ability to deliver. The following habits can also prepare your mind and body, help focus on the moment, and keep you from getting in your own way.

Physical preparation

Athletes physically warm up their muscles before each event. Basketball players physically warm up by shooting free throws and making shots from different areas of the court. Boxers shadow-box imaginary opponents. Runners get ready by running a short distance.

---

[2] Read the study at http://j.mp/pivotfear

Jumping jacks

Some actors like to warm up before an audition by shaking their entire body, starting from their hands. Many speakers do neck circles to loosen up their muscles. Other performers prefer to clap their hands together a couple of times and light up their faces with a big smile. In order to reduce his tension and raise his energy level, actor/comedian Robin Williams often did jumping jacks before going on stage.

Belly breathe

Make sure that you breathe optimally. If your breaths are deep, you can reduce your heart rate, calm yourself down physically, and increase the oxygen flow to your brain. This exercise also keeps you focused on the present, instead of worrying about the future.

To breathe with your diaphragm, place one hand on your abdomen and one hand on your chest. Breathe with your belly, while keeping your chest still. Your abdomen should move out as you inhale, and back in as you exhale.

Mental preparation

Mood music

Does listening to music lift your mood? Many athletes use songs as part of pre-game rituals to lower anxiety and get into "the zone." Their music playlists will surprise you:

- Eli Manning, two-time NFL Super Bowl MVP, listens to *This Is How We Do It* by Montell Jordan
- Jeremy Lin, the first Harvard graduate in the NBA since the 1950s, listens to *Cornerstone* by Hillsong
- Lebron James, two-time NBA Finals MVP, listens to *In The Air Tonight* by Phil Collins

Picture it

Can you imagine what it will look like to receive a standing ovation? Visualization is a powerful tool to help you focus on a successful outcome.

Jack Nicklaus, winner of 18 major champion-ships and considered the greatest golfer of all time, visualized every shot in his head before taking action:

> *It's like a movie. First I 'see' the ball where I want it to finish, nice and white and sitting up high on the bright green grass. Then the scene quickly changes and I 'see' the ball going there; its path, trajectory, and shape, even its behavior on landing. Then there is a sort of a fade-out, and the next scene shows me making the kind of swing that will turn the previous image into a reality.*[3]

Highlight reel

Can you remember a time when you were feeling at your best?

---

[3] Read the book at http://amzn.to/1SUYCfv

Think of your greatest past success. Remember the last time you were at the top of your game—from the sight, sound, touch, taste, and smell—and you'll vividly relive the experience in your mind and body. This technique generates trust in yourself, and enhances energy through positive reinforcement.

Picture your personal highlight reel and remind yourself: "I did it before, and I'll do it again!"

Cultivate the habit

Can you lock in a pre-event habit that combines both physical and mental preparation? Cultivate a brief routine that you go through immediately before you present, and keep focused on what's in front of you. Include a physical activity, such as jumping jacks, belly breathing, or power posing. Also include a mental component, such as a visualization of yourself succeeding, a loud ovation from your audience, or a personal highlight reel of your past success. Finish with a powerful trigger—either an action or phrase—to signal that you're ready for action!

If you want success in the future, start to achieve success in the present. Direct your focus to performing at your best right now. And be disciplined in your habits to get into the zone.

What will it take for you to channel your speaking anxiety into excitement?

Unstoppable speaking confidence begins with your physical and mental rituals. But that's not where it ends—especially if you want a professional reputation. Keep reading to discover why it's crucial to **Flip Your Focus**.

Each of us has a fire in our hearts for something. It's our goal in life to find it and keep it lit.

- MARY LOU RETTON

 **Activity**

(1) What will you do as your physical warm-up? Share your favorite exercise on Twitter, Facebook, Instagram and Pinterest using the hashtag **#ovationtip**

(2) What will you add to your warm-up music playlist? Share your favorite exercise on Twitter, Facebook, Instagram and Pinterest using the hashtag **#ovationtip**

(3) Visualize your success, as if you were experiencing it now. What will you see, hear, smell, taste, and feel?

(4) Describe your proudest moment, as if you were reliving it now. What did you see, hear, smell, taste, and feel?

(5) What will be your trigger to pivot from fear to excitement?

Chapter 2
Flip Your Focus

Communication does not begin with being understood,
but with understanding others.

- W. STEVEN BROWN

On a scale of 1 to 10, exactly how concerned are you with your audience?

Imagine you are standing on a stage. A giant spotlight is focused directly on your face. You feel hot and sweaty. You squint your eyes and see in front of you a sea of unfamiliar faces. Now imagine turning that spotlight away from you, and shining it on your audience.

Turn off that hot, sweat-inducing, nauseating moment— by flipping your focus from you, to your audience.

What are your audience's expectations? What do they know, what do they want to hear, and what don't they want to hear? Focus on *them*. Devote yourself to improving the condition of each person in the room. Shift your focus from "What's in it for *me*?" to "What's in it for *them*?"

Picture them as participants in a shared conversation. You make a statement or ask a question, and they answer verbally or physically. Pay attention to your audience, and your audience will pay attention to you.

From your audience to you

You'll feel good about yourself when you're of value to others. As actor Leonard Nimoy pointed out, "The more we share, the more we have."

Flipping your focus may begin with the audience, but then it comes back to you. And the better you feel, the more you can give. A strong self-esteem will help you bounce back whenever you face a presentation setback.

Self-esteem is more than a mere mental abstraction— it's broadcast from the inside out. Your self-worth shows up in your posture, your expression, and your voice. Feeling good about yourself is also the gift that keeps on giving. Recent research shows that higher self-esteem reduces the impact of anxiety.[4]

Unstoppable speaking confidence comes from within. You must have a strong belief in yourself, your message, and your industry/organization. On a scale of 1 to 10, how much do you believe in each one? What will it take

---

[4] See the study at http://j.mp/anxietybuffer

for you to score a perfect 10 in your beliefs?

Your first sale is always to yourself. If you don't buy what you're selling, you can't expect others to.

When many Americans first saw Bill Clinton on television, he put them to sleep! At the 1988 Democratic National Convention in Atlanta, the then-unknown Arkansas Governor was on the stage to endorse candidate Michael Dukakis. But Clinton was not audience-focused. His speech was so long and tiresome that when he finally said, "In conclusion," the audience burst into sarcastic cheers.[5]

Later describing the crowd's boos and jeers, Clinton said: "I just fell on my sword." But it was a valuable lesson, and "The Comeback Kid" had the confidence to persevere.

In 1992, Bill Clinton debated incumbent U.S. President George H.W. Bush and Ross Perot in a televised presidential town hall debate. When audience member Marisa Summers asked, "How has the national debt personally affected each of your lives?" Bush and Perot gave answers that were out of synch with the average American voter. Bush insisted that you don't have to be personally hit by a recession to know what it's like.

Then Clinton walked up to the audience member and engaged her in a conversation. He asked her how the recession had affected her. Clinton related to what

---

[5] Watch the video at http://j.mp/billclinton88

she said, and showed her that she had been heard and understood. Here's a portion of what he said next:

> *I've been governor of a small state for 12 years. I'll tell you how it's affected me. Every year Congress and the president sign laws that make us do more things and gives us less money to do it with. I see people in my state, middle-class people—their taxes have gone up in Washington and their services have gone down while the wealthy have gotten tax cuts.*
>
> *I have seen what's happened in these last four years when— in my state, when people lose their jobs there's a good chance I'll know them by their names. When a factory closes, I know the people who ran it. When the businesses go bankrupt, I know them.*
>
> *And I've been out here for 13 months meeting in meetings just like this ever since October, with people like you all over America, people that have lost their jobs, lost their livelihood, lost their health insurance.[6]*

Clinton's talk was a memorable moment. Throughout his presidential campaign, he continued to show his unstoppable speaking confidence and his laser-like focus on the audience. In 1993, Bill Clinton became the 42nd President of the United States.

Discover the secrets of Bill Clinton's powerful words in **Chapter 11: Lead With Language**. In the next chapter, you'll receive advice on how to *Keep Improving*.

---

[6] Watch the video at http://j.mp/billclinton92

This is who I am and I have value. And I hope you will accept it, but if you don't, I'm still good with who I am.

- MELLODY HOBSON

 Activity

(1) On a scale of 1 to 10, how concerned are you with your audience?

(2) Why are you speaking? Who are you speaking to, and how will they benefit?

(3) What do you know about your audience? What do you need to find out? Can you conduct surveys or make phone calls in advance, to help you understand them better?

(4) How can you create more value for your audience, through your presentation or supplementary materials?

(5) On a scale of 1 to 10, how strongly do you believe in yourself, your message, and your organization/industry? Do you have the full courage of your convictions?

Chapter 3
Keep Improving

In business or in football, it takes a lot of unspectacular preparation to produce spectacular results.

- ROGER STAUBACH

What's the worst that can happen when you present?

Did you see Transformers director Michael Bay speak at the 2014 Consumer Electronics Show? While appearing on behalf of Samsung, Bay and his teleprompter fell out of synch. He fumbled with his words and fidgeted with his hands. He said he was going to "wing it," but he didn't succeed. Thoroughly embarrassed, Michael Bay actually walked off the stage!

It's unlikely that Michael Bay rehearsed more than once—if that. But success often comes to those who do what others do not. As Bruce Lee said, "Knowing is not enough—we must apply. Willing is not enough—we must do."

From football players to Hollywood power players, elite performers need to practice. Even if you're a seasoned speaker, preparation is essential. If you plan in advance for what could go wrong, you're more likely to take unexpected situations in stride.

Take the time to prepare, and be confident that the next big public speaking meltdown probably won't be yours.

Practice, practice, practice

Bob Knight, the great American college basketball coach, once said: "The will to succeed is important, but what's more important is the will to prepare."

What does that mean for you as you prepare your next talk? Let's say you've done your background research and have created your presentation outline (covered in **Part Two: Deliver Unforgettable Messages)**. In other words, you're familiar with your audience and your venue, as well as the talk you plan to give.

Then you've used the simple techniques to remember your material (found in **Chapter 9: Speak Without Notes)**.

Now you're ready to do a dry run of your presentation. It will help you get more comfortable with your concepts, timing, and flow. Do a full presentation run-through and talk it through on your own.

The next step is to record and critique yourself. Use your smartphone to create a video or, at least, capture your voice while you speak. Try recording and re-watching yourself three times.

Once you feel more comfortable with your content, practice in front of a live audience. You'll gain more confidence in your material and your ability to adapt to the audience response. Consider giving your presentation to family, friends, coworkers, or your local chapter of Toastmasters.[7] Ask for feedback on your clarity, connection, and impact.

Always stay on time. In 1988, Bill Clinton's speech endorsing Michael Dukakis was twice as long as the time allotted, and the crowd booed him! Going over your time limit cuts into the schedule of the speakers or events after you, which is inconsiderate and unprofessional.

After practising so many times, are you afraid that you'll sound bored or mechanical? Refer back to the warm-up exercises in **Chapter 1: Lose Your Anxiety.** Like a professional athlete or actor, you must be in the moment each time you perform. As NBA Hall of Famer Jerry West observed, "You can't get much done in life if you only work on the days when you feel good."

It's always someone's first time hearing you speak, and they deserve your best effort. For extra motivation on

---

[7] Find a club at http://j.mp/toastmastersclubs

connecting to your audience, refer back to **Chapter 2: Flip Your Focus**. Do you believe in the message you're delivering? Is this message important to you? For extra motivation on connecting to your message, be sure to read **Chapter 4: Present With Purpose**.

Preview your venue

Research the place where you are scheduled to speak, as well as the event itself. How large is the venue, and how many people will attend your talk? Is there a microphone? If there's a microphone, is it handheld, a lapel, wireless, or attached to the podium? All of these factors will determine your speaking volume, the range of your movements, and the gestures you can make.

If you have slides, will you be able to see them without looking back at the screen? Will your audience be able to see them without your blocking the view? Remember to use media to enhance your presentation, not as memory tools.

When are you scheduled to speak on the agenda? If you're the opening speaker, you'll be expected to set the tone for the event and energize the audience. Speaking during or immediately after a large meal can be a challenge. The audience's attention is often focused on eating or digesting their food. Consider using an appropriate activity to get or maintain your audience's attention. Plan in advance.

Will your venue will have a countdown clock? As a professional, you must always end on time. Just in case, professional speaker Chris Cummins packs a light-weight laptop computer for his speaking engagements. He's installed an app that turns his device into a giant timer. Chris even uses his laptop to keep him on time when he emcees weddings![8]

If possible, practice on-site. Consider rehearsing the night before, or the morning of, your presentation. The ideal scenario would be to perform a full rehearsal on location with working audiovisual equipment, with the A/V team or a live audience. At a minimum, visit the venue beforehand so you know what to expect. Give yourself extra travel time, especially if you've never been there before.

Create a checklist

Create a checklist of what you need to bring for your presentation, from laptop to handouts. Update it after every presentation until all your bases are covered.

Here's what's on my checklist:

- Suit and tie
- Ironed dress shirt
- Polished shoes and matching belt
- Laptop and power cord
- Portable mouse
- Pointer device
- Presentation on laptop

---

[8] See more at http://j.mp/chriscummins

- Presentation on flash drive
- Extension cable
- Portable projector and screen (if needed)
- Portable speakers (if needed)
- Cell phone and charger
- Watch
- Business cards
- Handouts
- Printed presentation outline
- Products for sale and tracking sheet
- Newsletter sign-up form
- Speaking contract (for professional engagements)
- Printed introduction (two copies)
- Printed address of the venue
- Contact info, including cell phone number, for the organizer

Keep it in perspective

Don't be a perfectionist. Don't aim to be perfect—aim to be excellent. Perfectionists are too afraid of making mistakes. They often don't move forward because they don't feel they are ready yet.

"Discipline is the bridge between goals and accomplishment," said success expert Jim Rohn. Set measurable goals and aim for continuous improvement. After each presentation, reflect on what went well, what could have gone better, and how you could improve next time. Solicit feedback from the organizer and your audience.

In every field, top professionals count on coaches to

improve their performance. As Microsoft founder Bill Gates advises, "Everyone needs a coach. It doesn't matter whether you're a basketball player, a tennis player, a gymnast, or a bridge player." Olympic athletes work with Olympic coaches. Similarly, a trusted speaking coach will help you gain insight, avoid frustration, and achieve faster results.[9]

As achievement expert Brian Tracy says, "No one lives long enough to learn everything they need to learn starting from scratch. To be successful, we absolutely, positively have to find people who have already paid the price to learn the things that we need to learn to achieve our goals."

Though not the only component to mastery, an important factor for speaking success is deliberate practice.[10] Rehearse your presentation for just one hour and you will already see progress.

That said, no matter how much you prepare, your talks will not always go as planned. When you face speaking setbacks, never take them personally. Instead, be flexible and open to adjusting your goals and strategies as needed. Will there be other opportunities to give more effective presentations in the future? Most likely.

Learn to make every presentation you deliver better than before. Keep moving toward your goals and you'll keep getting better results.

[9] Get free tips for your presentations at http://rhtsang.com
[10] Read the research at http://j.mp/10khoursstudy

I've missed more than 9,000 shots in my career.
I've failed over and over and over again in my life.
And that is why I succeed.

- MICHAEL JORDAN

 Activity

Compare your most recent presentation with your best presentation ever, and answer the following questions:

(1) What worked well and why?

(2) What could have gone better and why?

(3) What feedback did you receive after your presentation or rehearsal?

(4) On a scale of 1 to 10, how would you rate your preparation and why?

(5) On a scale of 1 to 10, how would you rate your impact and why?

(6) On a scale of 1 to 10, how would you rate your connection and why?

Part Two:
Deliver
Unforgettable
Messages

Chapter 4
Present With
Purpose

You can't hit a target that you can't see.
- BRIAN TRACY

Do you want to save time and avoid frustration?

It's much easier to travel when your car or smartphone has a GPS. Even if you go in the wrong direction, your navigation system will tell you how to get back on track. But there's a question that your GPS always needs an answer to: where are you going?

Whether you travel or prepare a presentation, without a destination and a plan you could walk in circles. Random efforts lead to random results. Before you speak, do you have a clear vision of who will be in your audience, what do you want them to do, and why?

Begin with the end

To maximize your impact, begin with the end in mind.

It's easier to align each message and talking point when your objectives are clear. Even if you get distracted or taken off course when speaking, you can steer your presentation back on track when you know your destination. And after you present, you can objectively measure your success.

Your audience will fall into one of three categories:

(1) They like you, or agree with you

(2) They are neutral to you, or will be neutral to your message

(3) They don't like you, or don't agree with you

Your presentation will be more productive if you focus on reaching people in the first two categories.

Learn more about your audience before you speak. The more you understand about their work environment, how they spend their free time, and what stresses they face, the more relevant you can become. What are their expectations? After you speak, what do you want them to think, feel, or do differently?

Your research may include asking questions of the meeting organizer. For example, what is their ideal outcome? Find out who has presented in the past, as well as what worked and what didn't. You could also have informal conversations with audience members beforehand, or use surveys.

Are you ready to give your next talk? As you begin to prepare your presentation, I promise you that the process will be straightforward. The complexities of writing your speech have been divided into bite-size, manageable pieces. The book's end-of-chapter activities and **The Ovation Outline for Speeches™** will remove a great deal of the uncertainty and anxiety out of deciding what to say, and how to say it.

In the Activity section, you'll gain clarity on your presentation goals in order to achieve the results you desire. You'll start with Who, then ask yourself Why, When, and What. This will help you develop your **Presentation's Purpose**. Then you'll be able to create your next talk easily, using **The Ovation Outline for Speeches™**.

The Ovation Outline for Speeches™, is a template you can use to create your next presentation.

You'll start by thinking about your **Presentation's Purpose**, the **Core Message** of your presentation, and how to **Begin With a Bang**.

You'll get into your **First Talking Point,** with one to three supporting examples, followed by your **Second Talking Point** with one to three supporting examples, and your **Third Talking Point** with one to three supporting examples.

Then you'll think about how to **Summarize** your presentation, as well as how to **End With Excellence**. Also, you'll consider your **Memorable Moment**.

And that's the **The Ovation Outline for Speeches™**.

Download an electronic copy of **The Ovation Outline for Speeches™** template at rhtsang.com/book

Good speaking is clear thinking made audible.
- BILL WHEELER

 **Activity**

(1) Who are you speaking to?

(2) Why should they listen to you?

(3) What do you want your audience to think as a result of your talk?

(4) What do you want your audience to feel as a result of your presentation?

(5) What do you want your audience to do after you finish speaking?

The Ovation Outline
for Speeches™

You can create your next talk easily with this step-by-step guide. With each chapter in **Part Two**, you will progressively complete parts of **The Ovation Outline for Speeches™**. Start by filling out your **Presentation's Purpose**.

(1) What is your **Presentation's Purpose**?

_____

_____

Chapter 5
Master Your
Message

*If you can't explain it simply,
you don't understand it well enough.*

- ALBERT EINSTEIN

Ask yourself this question: "What is my talk really about?"

If you can't answer this question in 12 words or less, unfortunately, your premise is as clear as mud. If *you* can't explain what your talk is about, then how can *your audience*? Refer to **The Ovation Outline for Speeches™** and keep refining your **Core Message**.

Are you trying to say too much for your audience to understand, remember, and repeat? A confused audience won't act, so your presentation may not have the desired impact.

Dazzle your audience with your smile and make them laugh with your stories. But your **Talking Points** and your **Supporting Examples** must relate back to your **Core Message**. If your audience doesn't understand the point of your presentation, nothing will stick.

Create a **Memorable Moment** and make your message stick. Repeat a catchphrase, visual motif, or signature gesture that stays with your audience. Answer this question: "What do I want my audience to remember after my talk?"

When U.S. President Abraham Lincoln delivered the Gettysburg Address, he did not start by saying: "87 years ago, the Declaration of Independence was signed." Instead, he said: "*Four score and seven years ago*, our fathers brought forth on this continent a new nation, conceived in liberty, and dedicated to the proposition that all men are created equal." Now that's a **Memorable Moment**!

SNAP!

Your audience should understand and repeat important parts of your presentation. Make these parts more memorable. Make sure that your **Core Message**, and if possible, your **Memorable Moments,** have **SNAP**.

SNAP is an acronym for:

Short: Make it 12 words or less—it's easier to understand and remember

New: Create a sentence that has novelty

Action-oriented: Make the audience feel it, believe it, or do it

Purposeful: Relate your presentation back to its purpose or objective

The following slogans may inspire you to craft your own messages with **SNAP**:

- "Just do it."
- "Yes we can."
- "I have a dream."
- "The happiest place in the world."
- "Because I'm worth it."

Simplicity is the ultimate sophistication.
- LEONARDO DA VINCI

 **The Ovation Outline for Speeches™**

(1) What is your **Presentation's Purpose**?

_____

_____

(2) What is your **Core Message**?

_____

_____

Chapter 6
Begin With A Bang

The secret to getting ahead is getting started.
- MARK TWAIN

How long does it take for someone to form a first impression?

Less than a second. Research shows that it takes a split second for your audience to judge you, your character, and your personality.[12]

As humorist Will Rogers said, "You will never get a second chance to make a first impression." Strive to make a positive first impression. Think of your time on the platform: what will you do to start off on the right foot?

First Glance

Consider your bio, your presentation title or description, and your physical appearance. What would

---

[12] Read the research at http://j.mp/ablinkofaneye

your audience expect to hear from you? What would they not expect to hear?

When the audience first sees you, will you send the message that you want to convey? Many speakers decide to wear a full suit or blazer to show either authority or respect. Either dress to fit in—or choose to stand out. There are merits to both.

UnMarketing President Scott Stratten chooses to stand out. Scott typically shares the professional speaking stage with men wearing suits and ties. But he stands out in his black golf shirt and jeans. I've seen Scott give keynotes at several large business conferences and his message is always aligned with his authentic personal identity. In a recent conference photo with other keynote speakers in dark suits and ties, Scott stood out in his red t-shirt, holding up a cat.[13]

First Sentence

Use a powerful and relevant opening. An interesting hook encourages your audience to keep listening. Instead of saying, "So what?" your audience should be thinking, "Yes," "Wow," or "Me, too."

As Harvard professor Amy Cuddy points out, "You must be able to show them that you understand them—and, better yet, that you can relate to them. If they don't trust you, your ideas are just dead in the water. Having

---

[13] See the difference? http://j.mp/scott-unsuit

the best idea is worth nothing if people don't trust you."

An effective way to show that you understand and relate to your audience is to start with a spontaneous opening sentence or story. The purpose of this opening remark is to bond with your audience by referring to a common experience. Share a relevant comment about the occasion, location, meeting theme, previous speakers, your introduction, or the audience themselves. Or based on your bio, presentation title/description or your most obvious physical characteristic, tell the audience that you know what they're thinking. For example:

Sample Opening Sentence: "I know what you're thinking: how can a person as skinny as me possibly be a good chef?"

Sample Opening Sentence: "Thank you, Ron. It's true that I'm the CEO of an 8-figure business. What you don't know is that I was once homeless, and I lived in a van, down by the river!"

Sample Opening Sentence: "I love speaking here in Niagara Falls. Every time I visit, the waterfalls remind me I need to drink more water!"

Your hook could also be a fun fact, a startling statistic, or a provocative challenge. For example:

Sample Opening Sentence: "Writing down three good things every day increases happiness and decreases depressive symptoms!"

Sample Opening Sentence: "Here's something you may not know about the CIA: in the 1960s, they spent 5 years and $20 million to use cats as spies!"

Sample Opening Sentence(s): "In other industries, sales growth and profit margins are collapsing due to piracy and an 'indie mindset.' It's up to you to keep the same thing from happening to our industry!"

No matter how you choose to begin, the audience needs to relate to you and your talk right away. Make a compelling first impression.

First "A-ha"

Another option: if you use slides, start with an image that connects to your topic and attracts your audience's attention. Pause for a second to allow the visual to sink in, and continue with the rest of your presentation. You could also take a lesson from Hollywood and start with a story. For example, James Bond movies always start with an action scene that's related to the main plot.

You have many options to open your presentation. The intent is to give your audience a reason to stay and listen to the rest of your talk. How long should your opening be? A rule of thumb is that the length of this introduction should be 10 percent of length of your entire presentation.

Research your audience and their needs in advance, so that you have material that would interest them.

Consider referring to **Chapter 2: Flip Your Focus**.

Once you pique your audience's curiosity, it's up to you to maintain this momentum. Share your **Core Message** and your **Presentation's Purpose**. In addition, tell your audience how they're going to benefit. If appropriate, discuss your agenda, timing, and when you'll take questions. Then launch into your **Talking Points**.

Will your non-verbal communication detract from your message? To hear more about optimizing your sound, tune into **Chapter 13: Talk Loud and Clear**. To see how you might use your body language, head to **Chapter 14: Engage With Body Language**.

Download **The Ovation Outline for Speeches™** template at rhtsang.com/book.

Be sincere. Be brief. Be seated.

- FRANKLIN ROOSEVELT

 Activity

(1) What do you know about your audience, the occasion, and the event? How can you find out more?

(2) What are your audiences' expectations based on your bio, the title of your presentation, and your physical appearance? Ask a friend or colleague to help you with this exercise.

(3) Same as for question 2, but what *wouldn't* they expect to hear? Ask a friend or colleague to help you with this exercise.

(4) What can you say that connects you with the audience, and shows that you're connected in the moment with your audience?

(5) How will the audience benefit from your presentation?

 **The Ovation Outline
for Speeches™**

(1) What is your **Presentation's Purpose**?

_____

_____

(2) What is your **Core Message**?

_____

_____

(3) How will you **Begin With a Bang**?

_____

_____

Chapter 7
Position Your Points

How well we communicate is determined not by how well we say things but how well we are understood.

- ANDY GROVE

The main structure for your car is its chassis, and the main structural support for your home is its frame. What is the organizational structure of your presentation?

Make it easier for your audience to understand, believe, and remember what you say. Write down your ideas in **The Ovation Outline for Speeches™**. Use this template to express your thesis, provide logical support, and connect your ideas with a natural flow.

Rule of Three

Western audiences prefer a three-part narrative structure. They find humorous patterns in threes. They may even remember only three things from your presentation.

As a result, your material will more clear and effective

if you can convey it in three parts.

The Ovation Outline for Speeches™ includes three **Talking Points.** Your **Talking Points** are your presentation's three biggest takeaways, which must support your **Core Message**.

Each **Talking Point** is backed up by one to three **Supporting Examples**. Your **Supporting Examples** provide persuasive evidence for each **Talking Point**.

Persuade with purpose

According to the Greek philosopher Aristotle, there are three ways to persuade your audience to think, feel, and take action. Convince your audience by:

1. Using your credibility in your subject area
2. Making them think
3. Touching their hearts

Persuasive communication combines emotion, logic, and proof that you are an expert on your topic. Include your qualifications if they relate to the audience and your talk. Your qualifications, accomplishments, and testimonials sound more impressive when they are delivered by someone else, such as your introducer.

Use appropriate statistics, analogies, stories, case studies, testimonials, quotations, questions, and activities to back up your **Talking Points**. Use a variety of

Supporting Examples.

Different audiences may need different approaches. For example, statistics appeal to people who prefer logic and facts. Stories connect with people's emotions. Studies show that people who are more empathetic are more easily swept away by stories. But some people only relate to stories if they can see themselves in that situation.[14]

Different audiences have different needs, so try to understand who your typical audience member is. Based on your audience research, choose a persuasive blend of stories and figures for your **Supporting Examples**.

Are you curious to know how Hollywood writers, novelists, and advertisers tell compelling stories? You'll benefit from reading **Chapter 10: Share Your Stories**.

Transition smoothly

Just as each chapter in a book flows from the previous chapter, you should make a clear transition between each **Talking Point**. An excellent bridge between your points is to ask a rhetorical question, such as: "Now that we've attracted a flood of new prospects, how can we convince them to do business with us?"

Finish strong

Organize your list of **Talking Points** so that your

---

[14] Read the research at http://j.mp/storymagnet

last point is the most powerful. You should follow the same order of importance for your list of **Supporting Examples**. Start with your second best point and include your weakest point in the middle. Your ending leaves a lasting impression.

Presentation outlines

The Ovation Outline for Speeches™ can be used for presentations of any length. Scale the level of detail up or down, based the available time. Here are a few examples.

Example 1: The Full-Day Seminar

Let's say that your **Core Message** is:

Thought leaders can use digital marketing to massively grow their business.

If you're giving a *full-day* seminar, your **Talking Points** and **Supporting Examples** might look like this:

Talking Point 1:

Get a flood of prospective clients.

- **Supporting Example 1:**
  Create viral content—40-minute session.
- **Supporting Example 2:**
  Write effective sales letters—40-minute session.
  Supporting Example 3:
  Use paid advertising—40-minute session

Talking Point 2: *Turn prospects into paying clients.*

- **Supporting Example 1:**
  Build successful funnels—40-minute session.
- **Supporting Example 2:**
  Create video sales letters—40-minute session.
- **Supporting Example 3:**
  Cultivate email lists—40-minute session.

Talking Point 3: *Scale your business to eight-figures.*

- **Supporting Example 1:**
  Set goals for your team—40-minute session.
- **Supporting Example 2:**
  Get access to capital—40-minute session.
- **Supporting Example 3:**
  Form strategic relationships—40-minute session.

On the other hand, if you're giving a *45-minute* talk, you need to narrow your scope.

Example 2: The 45-Minute Presentation

The **Core Message** for your *45-minute* presentation:

Thought leaders can use digital marketing to get a flood of prospective clients.

Talking Point 1: *Create viral content.*

- **Supporting Example 1:**
  Research your market—5-minute example.

- **Supporting Example 2:**
  Find out what works for everyone else—5-minute example.
- **Supporting Example 3:**
  Find out what people search for—5-minute example.

Talking Point 2: *Write effective sales letters.*

- **Supporting Example 1**:
  Grab their attention—5-minute example.
- **Supporting Example 2:**
  Demonstrate the results they want—5-minute example.
- **Supporting Example 3:**
  Make it easy for them to take action—5-minute example.

Talking Point 3: *Use paid advertising.*

- **Supporting Example 1**:
  Google AdWords advertising—5-minute example.
- **Supporting Example 2:**
  Facebook advertising—5-minute example.
- **Supporting Example 3:**
  YouTube advertising—5-minute example.

And if you're giving a *5-minute* talk, you should narrow your scope even further with your **Core Message** and **Talking Points**.

Example 3: The 5-Minute Presentation

The **Core Message** for your *5-minute* presentation:

Thought leaders can do market research to create viral content.

Talking Point 1: *Learn what your audience responds to.*

* **Supporting Example**:
  What your audience likes—2-minute example.

Talking Point 2: *Find out what's working for everyone else.*

* **Supporting Example**:
  What your competitors are doing—1-minute example.

Talking Point 3: *Comment, curate or create.*

* **Supporting Example**:
  Success stories—2-minute example.

Your presentation

Download your copy of **The Ovation Outline for Speeches™** template at rhtsang.com/book

Fill in **The Ovation Outline for Speeches™** and most of your presentation writes itself. But do you need help communicating your ideas without reading off your notes? Be sure to read **Chapter 9: Speak Without Notes**.

> *True eloquence consists of saying all that should be said, and that only.*
>
> **- FRANÇOIS DE LA ROCHFOUCALD**

The Ovation Outline for Speeches™

(1) What is your **Presentation's Purpose**?

_____

_____

(2) What is your **Core Message**?

_____

_____

(3) How will you **Begin With a Bang**?

_____

_____

(4) What is your **First Talking Point**? What are your one to three **Supporting Examples**?

_____

_____

_____

_____

(5) What is your **Second Talking Point**? What are your one to three **Supporting Examples**?

_____

_____

_____

_____

(6) What is your **Third Talking Point**? What are your one to three **Supporting Examples**?

_____

_____

_____

_____

Chapter 8
End With Excellence

Great is the art of beginning, but
greater is the art of ending.

- HENRY WADSWORTH LONGFELLOW

How will you conclude your presentation?

The words you say at the conclusion of your presentation can leave a lasting impression. But many speakers finish their talks with a fizzle. Plan instead to end with excellence.

Not every presentation has a Q&A, but if you plan to have one, tell the audience and the emcee that you'll answer questions *before* you make your closing remarks. Make it clear that after the Q&A, you will have the final say. I made the mistake once of ending my talk on Q&A. The final question threw me off track, and then the emcee cut me off! Never again.

Provide a recap

Before you conclude, restate your three **Talking**

Points by presenting a **Summary**. Can you remind the audience of your main takeaways? This signals to your audience that you are coming to the end of your talk.

How do *you* want others to remember your presentation? Summarize—making sure your talk finishes on a positive note—then end on your own terms.

Call to action

If you know the objective of your presentation, you should be aware of what you want your audience to think, feel or do. Conclude with a call to action that leaves your audience uplifted, focused, and ready to act. If you need to, go back and revisit **Chapter 4: Present With Purpose**.

Have the final say

This is the wrap-up you will deliver after the Q&A. Close off with one of your **Memorable Moments**. Tell a story or share a profound thought. Make sure it relates to your **Presentation's Purpose**, **Talking Points,** or **Core Message**.

If possible, try to provide thematic closure for your audience. Tie your conclusion back to the beginning, like drawing a circle. For example, in his famous *I Have a Dream* speech, Martin Luther King begins and ends with a reference to his main theme: freedom.

First Sentence:
"I am happy to join with you today in what will go

down in history as the greatest demonstration for freedom in the history of our nation."

Last Sentence:
"Free at last! Free at last! Thank God Almighty, we are free at last!"

Memorize your closing sentences word for word. Stay focused and *avoid introducing any new points*, especially if they weren't developed earlier. After you share your closing thoughts, it should be abundantly clear to your audience that this is the end.

As you develop your conclusion, remember that your final words leave a lasting impression. Always **End with Excellence**.

To talk well and eloquently is a very great art, but an equally great one is to know the right moment to stop.
- WOLFGANG AMADEUS MOZART

The Ovation Outline for Speeches™

By now you will have filled every blank in your presentation, except for the last two. Now it's time to describe how you will summarize, and how you will end with excellence.

(1) What is your **Presentation's Purpose**?

_____

_____

(2) What is your **Core Message**?

_____

_____

(3) How will you **Begin With a Bang**?

_____

_____

(4) What is your **First Talking Point**? What are your one to three **Supporting Examples**?

_____

_____

_____

_____

(5) What is your **Second Talking Point**? What are your one to three **Supporting Examples**?

_____

_____

_____

_____

(6) What is your **Third Talking Point**? What are your one to three **Supporting Examples**?

_____

_____

_____

_____

(7) How will you **Summarize**?

_____

_____

(8) How will you **End with Excellence**?

_____

_____

(9) What was your **Memorable Moment**?

_____

_____

Chapter 9
Speak Without
Notes

*People like a presenter they can relate to. And they like
a presenter who speaks from their own knowledge—
rather than a script.*

- OLIVIA MITCHELL

What's more engaging: taking part in a conversation or
listening to someone recite a speech?

Try not to read from your notes. The exception is if
you're giving a political speech or a corporate announce-
ment, where the public will scrutinize every word and
figure. Otherwise, say it, don't read it.

When your eyes look down at your pages, you do not
connect with your audience. When you read from
your notes, you may sound disengaged. You may also
miss important visual cues from your audience. For
example: are they paying attention to you?

If you try to memorize your speech, you might forget

your lines. And it takes work to memorize your entire talk. Worse yet, if you've completely committed your script to memory, your material might sound canned!

For the body of the speech, the best speakers don't memorize—they internalize. Make the effort to know your outline and it will definitely pay off. You'll be a more engaging speaker if you're fully present and make eye contact at key points. Relive your stories—rather than retell them—and you will draw your listeners into the experience.

Optimize the Memory Work

Memorize key points instead of remembering every line. You should also know your introduction and conclusion word for word. Make a strong first impression on your audience and leave a lasting memory. A GPS requires an origin and a destination. Likewise, you need to know exactly how your presentation will begin and end.

Here are three proven techniques to help you optimize your memorization.

Use sticky notes

Take a pad of sticky notes, and your copy of **The Ovation Outline for Speeches™**. Review your three **Talking Points** and their **Supporting Examples**. Take three sticky notes and, on each one, write down a key phrase that represents each **Talking Point.** Grab more sticky notes and, on each one, write down a key phrase that summarizes each **Supporting Example**.

Next, write down a key phrase on a separate sticky note that describes how you'll **Begin With a Bang**. Lastly, take another sticky note and write down a key phrase that describes how you'll **End with Excellence**.

After reviewing your sticky notes, you can summarize your presentation on **five sticky notes:**

1. **Begin With a Bang**
2. **First Talking Point**
3. **Second Talking Point**
4. **Third Talking Point**
5. **End with Excellence**

Don't memorize the body of your talk word for word— only the beginning and ending statements. You'll have a much easier time remembering five key presentation phrases.

Picture a palace

Are you having a hard time remembering your five key presentation phrases? Try the *memory palace* technique for rapid organization and recall.

1. **Visualize** your five key phrases represented as five images.
2. **Imagine** walking into a place that you know well, such as your home. Imagine going to five rooms in order, such as the entrance hallway, the living room, the dining room, the kitchen and the washroom.

3. **Place** the image that represents your key phrase in each room.

Associate your five key presentation phrases with the five rooms you walk through. (It doesn't have to be your home; it could be your office or a place in the neighborhood you know well.) You'll remember the key phrases when you take a walk through each room in your *memory palace* and see a familiar image.

Take a nap

Studies show that after learning new information, you can improve your memory by taking a power nap. Short-term memories in your hippocampus can move into long-term storage in your neocortex. All you need is a six-minute nap. Sometimes the best thing you can do to remember your presentation is to sleep on the job.[15]

What if you blank out?

If you ever happen to forget what you're supposed to say next, it's not the end of the world. Many audiences won't even realize that you lost track of your thoughts.

Just stop and focus on taking a deep breath. Be acutely aware of how it feels when you inhale and exhale.

If after a few seconds your key phrase still doesn't come to you, feel free to admit that you lost your place.

---

[15] Read the research at http://j.mp/shortnap

Consider asking your audience if they can tell you where you left off. If necessary, carry on with what you remember from your last **Talking Point**. Or make a transition and introduce the next **Talking Point**.

Practice, practice

Practice with a timing device. As a professional, you must always end on time. But schedules may change, and the speaker(s) ahead of you may take more or less time than expected. Just in case, be prepared to expand or contract your presentation. Plan in advance what you can add or remove, and do it gracefully.

Don't underestimate the amount of practice time you need before you deliver your talk. But minimize your time memorizing your talk by following these three tips:

1. Use five sticky notes to construct your palace
2. Take a strategic nap to reinforce your new content
3. Visit your memory palace and see if you can deliver your presentation start to finish

Follow these tips when practicing to speak effectively without notes.

The best way to sound like you know what you're talking about is to know what you're talking about.
- HARVEY MACKAY

Activity

(1) By now you will have filled every blank in **The Ovation Outline for Speeches™**. Now it's time to commit your introduction, summary, and conclusion to memory.

(2) Describe the five images you've stored in your memory palace, and how they are connected to the five phrases you wrote down on your sticky notes.

(3) Without looking at your cheat sheet or sticky notes, recite your five key phrases.

The Ovation Outline
for Speeches™

(1) What is your **Presentation's Purpose**?

_____

_____

(2) What is your **Core Message**?

_____

_____

(3) How will you **Begin With a Bang**?

_____

_____

(4) What is your **First Talking Point**? What are your
    one to three **Supporting Examples**?

_____

_____

_____

_____

(5) What is your **Second Talking Point**? What are your one to three **Supporting Examples**?

_____

_____

_____

_____

(6) What is your **Third Talking Point**? What are your one to three **Supporting Examples**?

_____

_____

_____

_____

(7) How will you **Summarize**?

_____

_____

(8) How will you **End with Excellence**?

_____

_____

(9) What was your **Memorable Moment**?

_____

_____

Part Three: Create Unbreakable Connections

Chapter 10
Share Your Stories

Most people are more deeply influenced by one clear, vivid, personal example than by an abundance of statistical data.

- ELLIOT ARONSON

Have you ever felt compelled to watch more than one episode of a TV show, back-to-back?

Recent surveys show that you're not alone. Over 60 percent of Netflix subscribers regularly binge-watch.[15] More than ever, viewers are becoming immersed in continuing episodes and even multiple seasons of a TV show. That's because they want not just a single-episode "slice" of the story—they want to experience the entire story arc.

You, too, can hook audiences by using stories effectively. Long before people could read and write, they would share fables, folktales and myths. When it comes down to it, people love stories. As a speaker,

---

[15] Read the study at http://j.mp/bingewatcher

if you want to connect, inspire, and persuade—tell a story.

What exactly is a story?

A story is a narrative with a clear beginning, middle, and end, often involving cause and effect.

It describes a time when one or more characters face an unanswered question or unresolved conflict. The story follows what happens as the characters seek an answer or a resolution.

Why should you tell stories?

Connect

At age 14, I made my first sale. My cheery neighbor Lester and I were members of the school band. He played the trumpet and I played the saxophone. We wanted to raise money to travel to an upcoming music competition, but I was too scared to sell anything. Lester convinced me to go door to door with him to sell boxes of chocolate-covered almonds.

After visiting a few houses, Lester suggested that we split up. He said, "We can cover more ground."

I worried about getting rejected, and not knowing what to say. After knocking on over a dozen doors, I heard many variations of "no thank you." And my fear turned into frustration.

I was about to call it quits and walk home when Lester convinced me to knock on one more door. He said, "It's just a numbers game! You've got to play the game!"

So I visited one last house. This time, I tried a different approach, and played a game. I asked questions that led to a story about why I was there: Have you heard of Turner Fenton Secondary School? Do you like music? Do you like chocolate?

The man who answered the door asked me, "Are you serious?" As it turns out, he had his own story: he was an alumnus from my high school! When he was a student, he had also played in the concert band. Not only did he buy a box of chocolate-covered almonds from me, he bought two!

I don't remember who won the music competition, but I do know that we raised enough money to get there. We knocked on many doors, but more of them stayed open once I used a story to establish a human connection.

Ultimately, people buy from people they like and trust. Sometimes that's also who they sell to.

Speaking coach Ven Virah has a long-time girlfriend who loves to cook. She's always wanted to own a high-performance blender: the Vitamix. But Ven is frugal and hesitates to buy it. Compared to other blenders, this one comes at a considerable price. Ven says, "When it comes to expensive purchases in a relationship, the closest thing to a wedding ring is a Vitamix!" But his girlfriend's birthday is coming up. Ven hems and haws. But with a "you only live once" outlook, Ven decides to bite the bullet.

He finds a Vitamix salesperson and he describes, in detail, his girlfriend and her yearning for this blender. Ven discloses his desire to make her birthday memorable, but kvetches about the price. After hearing Ven's story, the salesperson leans in and says: "Don't tell anyone I did this, okay?"

Ven saves 40 percent off the retail price and walks home with bonus accessories that are worth hundreds. That day, his story about his girlfriend has created a human connection. That's why Ven received more value than any of the other customers.

Inspire

In Paulo Coelho's *The Alchemist,* the main character embarks on a journey that initially seems impossible. But it eventually becomes probable. *The Alchemist* has inspired droves of readers to pursue their dreams. It illustrates how a great story, the protagonist's Personal Legend, can transport and transform your audience.

Can you make your audience feel as though they're experiencing what's happening in your story? Remind them of experiences from their own lives. Present an experience they might like to have in the future. Unlike quantitative information, stories can ignite the imagination and stir the soul.

Born in the Middle East, Tahani Aburaneh grew up in a refugee camp and faced adversity early in her life. At age 15, she got married to someone she had never seen and moved to a foreign continent. Despite her bewildering circumstances, she saw it as an opportunity to receive an education and to give back to her family.

But when Tahani became a single mother with two young children, she needed to support them. This cause motivated her to succeed in her real estate career more than she imagined. Early on, she struggled to consistently bring in new business without sacrificing time with her two children. Then Tahani discovered real estate investing, which she immediately fell in love with. Driven to help her clients, she set out to learn everything that she could about this field. Through her dedication and desire to learn, Tahani became one of Canada's most sought-after experts in real estate investing.

Today, Tahani runs a successful real estate investing brokerage and development company. She is the founder of the SIAC (Savvy Investor Agent Certification) training program for realtors. And she authored two real estate books, including Amazon bestseller Real Estate Riches and Savvy Investor Agent Guide. All proceeds from her latest book are donated to care.org, an organization that fights poverty in third world countries, especially among women. Tahani also speaks around the world to empower others with her story and expertise.

Tahani Aburaneh's life story is proof that anyone can build the life of their dreams. Invest in yourself, live with passion, and focus on helping others. Follow these lessons and you, too, can gain financial independence and achieve great success.

Persuade

Stories are persuasive. Once a message enters your subconscious mind, it has the ability to shape your beliefs.

Merlot was one of the most popular red wines in North America until the 2005 film *Sideways*. In the film, Paul Giamatti's wine-loving protagonist refused to drink merlot. Instead, he mostly praised the virtues of pinot noir. *Sideways* gained international attention through several Oscar nominations. There was a correlation, as sales of merlot immediately slipped and pinot noir surged. A decade later, merlot sales have yet to return to pre-2005 highs, due to the influence of a popular story.

Parables are powerful. For example, Pastor Don Noble once shared with his congregation a simple but effective story about a cookie jar.

Imagine that you want to have a cookie—wouldn't a delicious, freshly-baked cookie hit the spot right now? So you reach into a cookie jar, fumble around inside, and feel a cookie between your fingers. But you discover that you're stuck! You can't get your hand back out of the jar!

You twist your hand in different angles, grease the rim of the jar, and yank that jar as hard as you can. But you *really* want that cookie, so you don't give up and you don't let go.

Imagine that you actually get used having your hand in that cookie jar. It even becomes a symbol of pride. You take that cookie jar everywhere you go—to the office, to the grocery store, to the shower. And when you go sleep, it's with your cookie jar.

What are we clinging onto in our own lives? What happens if it doesn't serve us, but we refuse to let it go? We remain stuck—and it keeps us from being able to enjoy the present and embrace the future.

Remember that we always have a choice to release our grip—and let go of that cookie.

How can you craft a good story?

Give it structure

Eliminate much of the uncertainty and anxiety from your storytelling by using **The Ovation Outline for Stories™**.

As you craft your personal stories, divide them into three parts: Acts I, II, and III. Most movies, plays, and novels follow the same three-act structure:

- Act I: Setup
- Act II: Confrontation
- Act III: Resolution

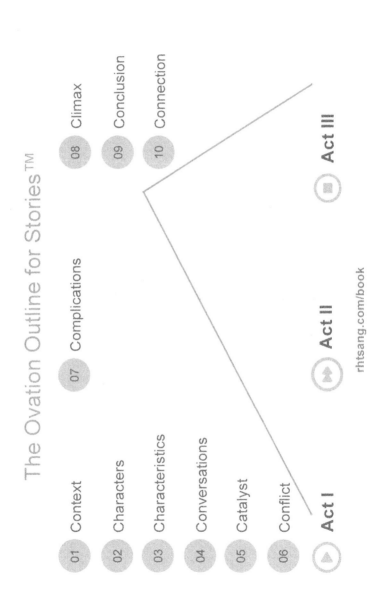

The Ovation Outline for Stories™

01 Context
02 Characters
03 Characteristics
04 Conversations
05 Catalyst
06 Conflict

07 Complications

08 Climax
09 Conclusion
10 Connection

Act I
Act II
Act III

rhtsang.com/book

In your Act I, introduce:

1. **Context:** Establish the time and location, where appropriate. For instance, in the movie *Star Wars*, we know that the story takes place "a long time ago, in a galaxy, far, far away."

2. **Characters:** Who is your story about?

   a. **Characteristics:** What do your characters look like, how do they act, and what would make one character different from another? For example, in the movie *The Godfather*, Sonny is hot-headed, while Michael is calm.

   b. **Catalyst:** Introduce the reason why your character(s) begin their adventure. For instance, in *The Wizard of Oz*, Dorothy is swept away from Kansas and begins a journey to return home.

   c. **Conversation:** Bring your characters to life using their words and voices. For example, early in the movie *Casablanca*, we learn more about Huphrey Bogart's character Rick when he says: "I stick my neck out for nobody!"

3. **Conflict:** Reveal what your characters want and why they want it—and what prevents them from getting it. For instance, in the movie *Rocky*, Sylvester Stallone plays an underdog boxer who's tired of being a nobody. To gain self-respect, he must go the distance in the boxing ring with world heavyweight champion Apollo Creed.

In your Act II, introduce:

1. **Complication:** Increase the tension in your story when things don't go as planned. For example,

in the *Mission Impossible* movies, a heist often goes wrong and someone is double-crossed.

In your Act III, introduce:

1. **The Climax:** Describe what happens when your characters finally confront their obstacles. As Rocky goes 15 rounds against his nemesis Apollo Creed, the story reaches its peak.

2. **The Conclusion:** Explain what happens as a result of the final confrontation. For example, by the end of the movie *The Wizard of Oz*, Dorothy returns home to Kansas.

3. **The Connection:** Make sure that your story has a point that relates back to your presentation.

Follow these guideposts and your story will progress like a rollercoaster. The stakes will get higher—until the story reaches a dramatic peak—and then it will finally come back down.

But here's another perspective. Award-winning Dallas Morning News columnist Dave Lieber developed a wonderful story structure. He calls it *Dave Lieber's V-Shaped Storytelling Formula*.

Imagine the letter "V." At the bottom of the letter V is a low point. Your goal as a storyteller is to bring your audience to this dip as soon as possible. As much as you can, dwell on your struggle in the low point before you finally rise up.

As Dave Lieber explains it, you don't learn from success; you learn from failure.[16]

Make it concrete

Tell a story and make it relate to a point in your presentation. Good storytellers want audiences to feel what they feel when telling a story. Make your story unforgettable by reliving a compelling experience that your audience can identify with, and connect it to an underlying message.

Hall of Fame trial lawyer Moe Levine sought compensation for a client who had lost both arms in an accident. His closing arguments painted a brief but tragic image:

> *As you know, about an hour ago we broke for lunch. I saw the bailiff come and take you all as a group to have lunch in the jury room. Then I saw the defense attorney, Mr. Horowitz. He and his client decided to go to lunch together. The judge and court clerk went to lunch. So, I turned to my client, Harold, and said "Why don't you and I go to lunch together?" We went across the street to that little restaurant and had lunch. [Significant pause.] Ladies and gentlemen, I just had lunch with my client. He has no arms. He has to eat like a dog. Thank you very much.[17]*

Moe Levine's client won one of the largest settlements in the history of the State of New York.

---

[16] Learn more at http://j.mp/davelieber
[17] Read more at http://j.mp/lawyerstory

A good story is fresh, with rich characters, and unexpected elements or details. Your audience will not remember every single word you say. But they will remember what they see and feel while they listen to you speak. Lawyer Moe Levine did not say something as bland as, "My client has a low quality of life." Instead, he used an unforgettable image—that of a human being who needs to stick his face inside a bowl in order to eat. Make your descriptions sensory-rich and concrete.

You don't get a standing ovation by just sharing statistics. People rationalize facts and figures, but stories touch the heart. Your audience might think with their head, but it's often their heart that inspires them to action.

Ensure it's relatable

Psychologists believe there are four basic human emotions. They include the following:[18]

1. Happiness
2. Sadness
3. Fear/surprise
4. Anger/disgust

A good story evokes at least one of these four emotions.

In the movie *Die Hard,* off-duty New York City Police Department officer John McClane is trapped

---

[18] Read the research at http://j.mp/fourfeelings

in a building taken over by terrorists. On top of the conflict of good versus evil, what's really at stake in the story is whether John McClane will get back together with his wife.

First-time action star Bruce Willis portrayed John McClane as an ordinary human being with some rough edges. John McLane is alone against overwhelming odds, and is someone who could actually lose. Over 25 years later, *Die Hard* is still a contender for the greatest action movie of all time. The compelling story, the relatable characters, and novel elements like the scramble through an elevator without power, make it a memorable movie.

A good story is one that will pull in your audience, create an emotional response, and connect to a take-away point, or lesson. Will your audience relate to your characters' motivations, as well as how they think and feel? A good story contains conflict, and something of consequence at stake.

People love stories. Stories can change minds, touch hearts, and shape beliefs. Adding storytelling to your presentations to yield remarkable results.

How to keep track of your stories

Create a story file that includes your favorite stories, works in progress, and key points you write down in **The Ovation Outline for Stories™**. Find interesting stories based on what you read, hear, and experience.

For easy access through digital devices, consider storing your story file in the cloud. Categorize stories based on a universal lesson, emotion, or context (such as the location). You never know when you'll find an opportunity to share these stories next.

> *Tell me a fact and I'll learn. Tell me the truth and I'll believe. But tell me a story and it will live in my heart forever.*
>
> **- INDIAN PROVERB**

 Activity

(1) What is your favorite or most important story from your life, your organization, or your industry, and why?

(2) If you knew you were going to die tomorrow, what advice would you want to share? How did you learn it: through experience, or from someone telling you?

(3) Do these stories relate to the core message in your presentation or a key talking point?

(4) How can you add rich sensory details to your stories: such as what you saw, smelled, tasted, heard, and felt?

(5) Will your stories match your audience's beliefs, values, and experiences?

The Ovation Outline for Stories™

(1) What is the **Context**?

(2) Who are your **Characters**?

(3) What are their **Characteristics**?

(4) What is their **Catalyst**?

(5) Can you voice their **Conversations**?

(6) What is the **Conflict**?

(7) What is the **Complication**?

(8) What happens at the **Climax**?

(9) What happens at the **Conclusion**?

(10) What is the **Connection** to your presentation?

Chapter 11
Lead With
Language

The art of communication is the language of leadership.

- JAMES HUMES

Do you speak like a leader?

Leaders need to lead by example, as well as through their words. Use words and phrases strategically. They get your audience's attention, make them think, and touch their hearts.

Use more "you"

As discussed earlier, it's important to bring value to your audience. Your choice of words conveys how concerned you are with your audience's needs. With that in mind, one of the most important words to use is "you."

Build stronger connections with your audience by including them in your words. Focus on what's in it for them. For example:

Ordinary:

"Let's talk about the three-act Hollywood storytelling formula, which includes characters, conflict, and climax."

Better:

"In the next 45 minutes, you'll learn: how to distill your story into three parts so it's easier for your audience to understand; how to establish characters that your audience will care about; how to keep your audience's attention by increasing the intrigue; and how to make the outcome feel satisfying to your audience."

There are many opportunities for you to switch your focus from "I" to "you." For example:

Ordinary:

"My dad always taught me that 'I can always learn something from anyone.'"

Better:

"I don't know what advice you received from your dad, but mine always said: 'You can always learn something from everyone.'"

Phrases such as "you guys" and "all of you" suggest that you're speaking to the entire room. While that's true, your audience is actually made up of individual human beings. Build a stronger connection with each person in the room to sound like you're speaking one-to-one. Start by replacing variations of "you all" with "you."

For your reference, U.S. President John F. Kennedy's famous inaugural address ("ask not what your country can do for you—ask what you can do for your country") used the words "you" and "your" 10 times, and "we" 30 times. But he used the word "I" fewer than five times.[19]

Word order

Which phrase sounds more powerful, A or B?

> A: Death and taxes are the only certain things in life.
> B: The only things certain in life are death and taxes.

You can change the emphasis of a sentence simply by rearranging the words. Think of each sentence as three parts: the beginning, the middle, and the end. Position your words in such a way as to amplify your audience's understanding and retention.

Consider beginning your sentence with context or known information. When appropriate, end your sentence with important or new information. That includes starting with "set up" words and finishing with "impact" words.

Words related to time are common set-up words, misused as impact words. These examples show that when time-related phrases are used as set-up ideas, sentences become more impactful:

---

[19] Hear the speech at http://j.mp/jfkbegins

A: "I will climb Mount Kilimanjaro in September."
B: "In September, I will climb Mount Kilimanjaro."

A: "This will be our focus for the next 24 hours."
B: "For the next 24 hours, this will be our focus."

Words at the end of a sentence carry the most weight. Impact words are action-oriented or make an emotional connection. For instance, which sentence sounds more positive?

A: "We exceeded our monthly revenue targets, though we lost key personnel."
B: "Though we lost key personnel, we exceeded our monthly revenue targets."

Concrete vs. abstract

Effective speakers combine big picture, strategic concepts with relatable, tactical examples. Take your speaking to the next level by understanding when to be abstract, and when to be concrete. Words such as "truth," "justice," and "freedom," are examples of abstract language. These intangible, symbolic ideas are only understood intellectually. In contrast, words that resonate with one or more of the five senses are examples of concrete language. For example the following phrases are understood, "a crisp twenty-dollar bill," "freshly baked bread," and "an obese orange tabby cat."

It's dangerous to use only abstract or only concrete phrases. A politician who speaks only about high-concept policies, without providing concrete examples, is confusing, or at best, unclear. A software engineer who communicates only low-level technical details, but doesn't explain the relevance, is boring.

To make your talk more abstract: give the 10,000-foot view, outline your broad strategy, and share your ideals or first principles. However, abstract phrases can be vague, uninteresting, and forgettable. To make your language more concrete, use a mixture of sensory language, stories/anecdotes, and specific examples.

If your audience can imagine it, they can believe it. When referring to abstract principles, add concrete details to make your presentations memorable.

You can also illuminate a point and reinforce a message by triggering your listeners' sensory memory. Consider the following examples:

- Sensory neutral: "Do you understand?"
- Visual: "Do you see what I mean?"
- Auditory: "Does that sound about right?"
- Kinesthetic: "Did you catch the gist of it?
- Olfactory: "Did that pass the smell test?"
- Gustatory: "Wasn't that sweet?"

Great leaders provide a clear view of what the future should look like. Paint a vivid word picture of your vision for tomorrow, and people will see it in their mind's eye today. The unknown future becomes grounded in certain reality.

Which statement sounds more powerful?

A: Someone who didn't read this book: "Let's go into space."
B: Former U.S. president John F. Kennedy: "By the end of the decade, we will put a man on the moon."

A: Someone who didn't read this book: "One day, I hope there are a lot of computers."
B: Bill Gates (in 1977): "A computer on every desk and in every home."

A: Someone who didn't read this book: "Can't we all get along?"
B: Martin Luther King: "I have a dream that my four little children will one day live in a nation where they will not be judged by the color of their skin, but by the content of their character."

Not surprisingly, research supports the benefits of using sensory-filled words. U.S. presidents who used image-rich words in their speeches were considered to be more charismatic than those who didn't.[20] Capture the imagination of your audience and motivate them to action by using evocative language.

Compare and contrast

Great speakers can explain an unfamiliar idea by showing how it's similar to a more familiar one. They can also clarify or give new meaning to an idea by comparing

---

[20] Read the research at http://j.mp/speechcharisma

it or contrasting it with another.

Consider this quote by Ernest Hemingway: "There is nothing noble in being superior to your fellow man; true nobility is being superior to your former self." The concept of your "fellow man" and "former self" are deliberately compared.

Contrast and repetition make this sentence stronger and more memorable than this shorter version: "True nobility is being superior to your former self, not just to other people."

University of Toronto professor Ramy Elitzur teaches MBA-level accounting courses with an approach he calls "The Accounting Art of War." Managers strategically manipulate financial statements, so Ramy compares financial accounting to modern warfare. He quotes *The Book of Family Traditions on The Art of War:* "Appearance and intention are fundamental to the Art of War... the strategic use of ploys, the use of falsehoods to gain what is real." By drawing on Chinese generals and Japanese samurai, Ramy turns abstract concepts from financial accounting into lessons that are concrete and relatable.

As Martin Luther King said, "With this faith, we will beable to hew out of the mountain of despair a stone of hope. With this faith we are able to transform the jangling discords of our nation into a beautiful symphony of brotherhood."

During a bleak time in U.S. history, contrast and repetition persuaded many Americans that widespread racial intolerance could one day be overcome.

Repetition

As demonstrated in the previous examples, repetition is an important persuasive tool. As demonstrated again in this sentence, repetition is an important persuasive tool. Why would you choose to restate the same word or phrase? Repetition adds rhythm and reinforces a message. As an example, Martin Luther King's famous speech echoes the phrases "I have a dream" and "Free at last" to add attention and importance.

Revisiting the quote from Ernest Hemingway: "There is nothing noble in being superior to your fellow man; true nobility is being superior to your former self." Repeating the words "noble" and "superior" makes this sentence stronger than stating: "True nobility is being superior to your former self, not to other people."

In 1940, British Prime Minister Winston Churchill announced: "We shall fight on the beaches, we shall fight on the landing grounds, we shall fight in the fields and in the streets, we shall fight in the hills; we shall never surrender." In this statement, there was no question that he declared war.

Rule of Three

As introduced in **Chapter 7**, the Rule of Three is a

form of repetition, and exerts a powerful subconscious pull. Western audiences tend to:

- Prefer a three-act narrative structure
- Find humorous patterns in threes
- Remember only three things from your presentation

Your sentences often sound more convincing if you use a three-part structural pattern. Use the Rule of Three to convey a message, explain an idea, or draw a comparison.

For example:

- Julius Caesar famously boasted, "I came, I saw, I conquered."

- Former U.S. First Lady Eleanor Roosevelt stated: "Great minds discuss ideas. Average minds discuss events. Small minds discuss people."

- And as Poet Maya Angelou observed: "I've learned that people will forget what you said, people will forget what you did, but people will never forget how you made them feel."

If you have an important point to make, don't try to be subtle or clever. Use a pile driver. Hit the point once. Then come back and hit it again. Then hit it a third time—a tremendous whack.

- WINSTON CHURCHILL

 **Activity**

(1) How will you increase your references to "you" or "we" in your presentation?

(2) Can you change the word order in your key sentences, to increase your impact?

(3) What will you do to incorporate more sensory-rich language?

(4) How will you emphasize words more strategically?

(5) What ideas can you compare or contrast?

(6) Where can you use repetition or the Rule of Three?

Chapter 12
Hunt For Humor

From there to here, and here to there,
funny things are everywhere.

- DR. SEUSS

Do you consider yourself to be funny?

When you make your audience laugh, you create a spontaneous shared experience that makes them feel more connected to you and to each other. Humor breaks through tension and resistance, and makes presentations more fun. A little humor goes a long way.

But you don't need to be a stand-up comedian. Even if you don't consider yourself to be funny, you can find sources of humor that feel natural to both you and your audience.

Using others' jokes

When borrowing humor, always acknowledge the source. If it's recycled comedy, be especially sure to tell it well. If using someone else's jokes, though, consider that the audience may have heard it before. This could lessen your intended impact, reduce your audience's engagement, and lower your credibility.

Several years after U.S. Vice President Al Gore and U.S. Secretary of State Colin Powell left the White House, I heard them speak at two separate events. Each of them began their keynote with a whimper—by starting off with the exact same canned joke! Be careful when using borrowed jokes.

Find the funny

Your own personal stories are the best source for unique material, especially if they relate to your presentation. You can often uncover humor in your stories by reading each line and asking yourself how a comedic character would respond. Pick the most appropriate response for your audience.

For example, let's refer to the time I met Warren Buffett. He's one of the wealthiest people in the world, so what might a class clown say?

- My inner child would say: "Does he swim in a vault filled with gold coins, like Scrooge McDuck?"

- My sarcastic voice would say: "Does he have a daughter?"

- My other sarcastic voice would say: "You have another sarcastic voice?"

I added the first two questions to my "funny file," and used the first sarcastic quip in the **Introduction**. The joke about Warren Buffett's daughter is relatable to all of my audiences, from Toronto to Tokyo. Using the same process, you can "find the funny" in your material, too.

You can find out more about your own sense of humor by making a list of what, or who, you find funny. If knock-knock jokes or limericks make you chuckle, then consider using one if it fits your audience.

That said, you should also take note of what doesn't make you laugh, so you know what not to use. If you don't find certain jokes funny, how could you deliver them with confidence? Find humor in what you read and hear. Pay attention to jokes, quick-witted remarks and funny anecdotes, and save them in a document or folder. For me, that's my "funny file." The same goes for funny photos, Internet memes and videos. Keep them in one place so you can find them easily.[21]

Rule of three, revisited

Humor depends on contrast and surprise. Study popular jokes and you'll find that most have a three-part structure: (1) set-up, (2) continuation or complication, and (3) punch line. The third time's the charm.

The set-up describes the situation, the second part

[21] For example, watch this funny video involving pandas: http://j.mp/findinghumor

progresses the pattern, and the finale unexpectedly changes the pattern. The surprise or misdirection is often what's funny. For example, many classic jokes are based on three stock characters who share a common situation: "A priest, a rabbi, and a minister walked into a bar…" The first two characters react normally, then the third does something ridiculous but often stereotypical. Comedy gold. But over-use the Rule of Three and your audience will find it to be repetitive, tiring, and may mentally or physically walk out the door.

Be self-deprecating

Be willing to laugh at yourself. It shows that you don't hold yourself above your audience and makes you more endearing. Share an embarrassing experience or an observation about yourself if it applies to your subject or ties back to a key point. Ask yourself how your favorite comedian or funny fictional character might poke fun at you.

Find common ground

No matter how different you are from your audience, you have some things in common—at the very least, you are at the same event and in the same room (or are dependent on the same internet connection). Find something in common with your audience so you can pick subjects that you can both laugh about. For example, mention an appropriate current event or reference a well-known celebrity or famous figure. Once again, consider asking yourself what funny characters or professional comedians might say.

Be audience appropriate

When selecting from your humor file, consider how appropriate a joke is for your audience. Decide how suitable it is for the occasion, and how relevant it is to your presentation. As a speaker, your comic relief should help you connect, not alienate, your audience. As well, your choices of humor shouldn't cause you to lose face or credibility.

Practice

The best comedy is all about timing, and that's why practice is crucial. Stand-up comedians practice their routines extensively. Late-night television host Jimmy Fallon rehearses all of his opening comedy monologues in front of a live audience. If a joke gets a laugh, it's a keeper.

You can test out your jokes, remarks and funny stories with friends or at your local chapter of Toastmasters.[22] You can fine-tune the timing for maximum impact. If a joke gets a laugh, and you can tell it well, you have a keeper. Your confidence will make your delivery even more effective.

Weave humor into your material and make your audience laugh. You will go help to keep your audience's

---

[22] Find meetings at http://j.mp/toastmastersclubs

attention longer and add to their enjoyment. Their laughter will also bolster your confidence and boost your energy throughout the presentation.

Humor is mankind's greatest blessing.

- MARK TWAIN

 **Activity**

(1) Where will you keep your "funny file," and what will you add to it?

(2) What was the last thing you saw or heard that made you laugh? What made it funny? Was it contrast, surprise, or something else?

(3) In reviewing your material, when can you use the comedy Rule of Three? Use it sparingly, please.

(4) Who are the comedic characters you can channel to "find the funny" in your material?

(5) Where can you find comedic common ground with your audience?

Chapter 13
Talk Loud And Clear

You can speak well if your tongue can deliver the message of your heart.

- JOHN FORD

How do you come across when you speak, and is how you sound aligned with your message?

As a presenter, you must pay attention not just to your words but also to your voice. You seem confident, competent, and trustworthy—or not—based on how you sound. From 1960 to 2000, the winner of the popular vote from every U.S. presidential election was the candidate with the lower voice. It's critical to consider both what you say and how you say it.[23]

When preparing your presentation notes, make sure you write for the ear, not for the eye. Your audience has different expectations when they listen to, rather than read, your words. Using shorter words, and being more conversational, will help you connect

---

[23] Read the research at http://j.mp/usvoting

with your audience.

When speaking to your audience, you can sound dominant, deferential, or equal. You can sound engaged or aloof. You can sound like someone they want to listen to—or the opposite.

As a reminder to put your audience first, and to cultivate more powerful connections with them, refer to **Chapter 2: Flip Your Focus**.

Add vocal variety

Have you noticed that engaging speakers have vocal variety?

Monotonous speakers have a flat and boring voice, and lack the musicality of a rising or falling inflection, tonality, and volume. Audiences find it hard to connect with a speaker when everything sounds the same, and they'll often tune out. Fortunately, this can be changed through mindfulness, and with multiple exercises you can practice.

Record yourself on your smartphone, either with a voice memo or a video. If you've never heard how your voice sounds, this exercise is a must-do. Record yourself reading the next five sentences, emphasizing the words **in bold** and then play it back.

1. "You can speak well if your tongue can deliver the message of your heart."

2. "You can **speak well** if your tongue can deliver the message of your heart."

3. "You can speak well if your tongue can **deliver** the message of your heart."

4. "You can speak **well** if your tongue can deliver the **message of your heart.**"

5. **"You can speak well if your tongue can deliver the message of your heart."**

Does your voice sound as flat in sentence #1 as in sentence #5, as compared to the other sentences? It should. The key to vocal variety is emphasizing certain words, not all words.

To emphasize a word, change how you say it:

- Pause for a split second longer than usual before, and after.

- Let the word roll off your tongue slightly slower than usual.

- Get a tiny bit excited when you say it.

Drawing attention to important words makes it easier for your audience to understand and retain your message. For a quick refresher on word emphasis, flip to **Chapter 11: Lead With Language**. Also, practice the next exercise and the end-of-chapter activity.

Consider applying a more conversational style to your presentation. We naturally use vocal variety in our everyday discussions. Organize your thoughts using **The Ovation Outline for Speeches™**. Then speak to your audience the way you would if you were sitting at home, in a restaurant, or at a bar. Don't force yourself to mechanically deliver a presentation. Instead, have a conversation with your attendees.

Articulate and enunciate

Do people often ask you to repeat yourself? If so, you might be mumbling—speaking too indistinctly and quietly for others to hear—or you might be a rapper from Atlanta. Either way, I know how annoying it is to be constantly asked: *"What?"*

As a habitual mumbler in my teens, I discovered that mumbling happens when your mouth isn't open enough. If your teeth and lips are partially closed or your tongue doesn't move, your words won't come out clearly.

You can stop mumbling if you enunciate, articulate, and exaggerate. The following exercise will help you pronounce your sentences.

Repeat these sentences:

> *"I don't know who you are. I don't know what you want. If you are LOOK-ING for a RAN-SOM I can tell you I don't have MON-EY, but what I do have are a very PAR-TIC-U-LAR set of skills."* [24]

---

[24] Watch a demonstration at http://j.mp/takenspeech

Open your mouth wide and deliberately pronounce each syllable. Make a special effort to pronounce the final sound in each word, and use it to carry you to the next word. This ensures a consistent connection and flow between your words.

Pause for punctuation. Consider pausing one second for a comma and two seconds for a new sentence. Breathe between sentences, not during them.

You don't need to sound like actor Liam Neeson. But you do need to enunciate, articulate, and exaggerate. Repeat the sentences above with different emotions, such as happiness, sadness, and anger. Practicing this exercise will help you stop mumbling.

Speak louder

Have you been told that your voice is too soft? If you have a deep, muffled voice like I do, you also need to increase your volume. If your voice is quiet and hard to hear, this exercise will help you gauge and adjust your volume.

Get up to speak at the front of a room, and ask a friend or colleague to stand at the back. After you speak, write down what you thought your volume was on a scale of 1 to 10, and ask the other person to do the same. Compare notes. Are you quieter, or louder, than you thought?

To speak louder, repeat the exercise. But this time,

imagine turning up the volume of your stereo, smart-phone, or other music device—and increasing the projection of your own voice. Now slowly turn up the volume. Compare notes with your friend or colleague. Are you quieter, or louder, than you thought?

To speak more quietly, repeat the exercise, but imagine lowering your volume, instead.

Don't try to push your voice, which could make you hoarse and damage your vocal cords. Instead, expand it. Use your tongue to touch the roof of your mouth and use your finger to lightly push the back of your tongue. And imagine that the inside of your throat and mouth have grown as large as the room you're speaking in. Visualize a bigger space inside your throat, and you'll have a bigger voice outside.

To improve the carrying power of your voice, make sure that you breathe optimally. If your breaths are shallow, you will quickly run out of air. The muscles in your throat will tense up and squeeze out your sounds.

Place one hand on your abdomen and one hand on your chest. Breathe with your belly. Your abdomen should move out as you inhale, and back in as you exhale. Your chest should be still.

Avoid credibility killers

Many of us enjoy snacks such as cookies, chips, or ice cream. But since they give us little true nourishment, these foods are empty calories. Many of us also include empty calories when we speak. Reduce your verbal empty calories, and present with clarity, confidence, and credibility.

Filler words

Do you use a lot of filler words, also known as crutch words, or worse—verbal vomit? These unconscious verbal tics commonly slip into our sentences when we're buying time to think about what to say next.

The most common filler words include:

- Uh
- Um
- Like
- Y'know
- Like
- I mean
- So
- Basically
- Actually
- Honestly
- Just
- Literally

From your audience's perspective, verbal vomit adds no meaning, increases distractions, and signals uncertainty. It dilutes your message. When used excessively, verbal vomit kills your credibility.

How can you sound more credible, confident, and concise?

PAUSE.

Pause… and think, before you speak. Let the words simmer inside your head before they come out of your mouth. As Mark Twain noted, "The right word may be effective, but no word was ever as effective as a rightly timed pause."

Pause… and think, before you speak, and you will avoid verbal vomit.

Up-talk

Do you sound like a *valley girl?*

Up-talk is the speech pattern where most of your words or sentences sound like a question. This takes place when your sentences end with a rising pitch. "You know what I mean?" suggests a speaker who does not know what they mean.

If you speak using up-talk, you don't come across as authoritative. Instead, it sounds like you're double-checking everything. You sound uncertain, and the audience wonders whether it's worth their time to listen to you. To avoid up-talk, ensure that you end definitive sentences with a downward inflection.

Vocal fry

Beyond up-talk, do you speak with *vocal fry?*

As author Naomi Wolf describes it, "'Vocal fry' is that guttural growl at the back of the throat, as a Valley girl might sound if she'd been shouting herself hoarse at a rave all night." Many people now speak with this world-weary, creaky voice—particularly young women.[25]

Some speakers, especially women, lower their voice to sound more authoritative, and unintentionally speak with a croak. To avoid vocal fry: breathe with your belly, enunciate the end of your sentences, and slightly raise the pitch of your voice.

Exceptions

Unless it's accepted in your target industry and demographic, minimize filler words, up-talk, and vocal fry. It's seldom a good idea to sound distracting and uncertain, clueless and insecure, or world-weary and disinterested, but there are instances where you might want to exploit these very qualities.

Strong speakers cultivate vocal variety, and might want to add dialogue or characters. Up-talk, vocal fry, filler words: these can all be employed to good effect.

---

[25] Watch a demonstration at http://j.mp/vocalfried

Both your words and your voice must be aligned with the needs of your audience and the nature of your presentation. Improve the delivery and quality of your voice, and be the best version of yourself as you present.

There are three things to aim at in public speaking: first, to get into your subject, then to get your subject into yourself, and lastly, to get your subject into the heart of your audience.

- ALEXANDER GREGG

 Activity

(1) What do you want your audience to think or feel when you speak, and why?

(2) Do you want to come across as dominant, deferential, or as an equal? How does that come across in the sound of your voice?

(3) Does your voice convey the emotion you want it to?

(4) Complete the Speak Louder exercise. On a scale of 1 to 10, how loud is your voice? Does it match what others think?

(5) Complete the Articulate and Enunciate exercise using different emotions, such as happiness, sadness, and anger. On a scale of 1 to 10, how clear is your enunciation?

(6) Record yourself having a conversation about your favorite people, hobbies, and moments. Then record yourself talking about something you find ridiculously boring. Listen to both recordings. Did you hear a difference in your tonality? Conjure up that passionate feeling the next time you need to sound enthusiastic.

(7) On a scale of 1 to 10, how often do you use verbal fillers, up-talk, and vocal fry? How can you cut out the empty calories when you speak? Remove credibility killers from your regular conversations and you'll minimize them during your presentations.

Chapter 14
Engage With
Body Language

*Your body language, your eyes, your energy will come
through to your audience before you even start speaking.*

- PETER GUBER

Is your body language aligned with your message?

As a speaker, your body language is an orchestra. The
instruments in that orchestra include everything from
your head to your toes, but especially your face, your
hands, and your feet. Like listening to a musical ensem-
ble, your audience will notice if your instruments are
out of synch.

Control your body language and you'll control how
well you connect with your audience. When speaking
to your audience, you can look dominant, deferential,
or comparable to them. You can come across as engaged or aloof, confident or timid. To send the appropriate message, conduct your orchestra well. Play the

right tune, and play the tune right.

Remember that your audience doesn't know how you *feel.* They only know how you *appear.* With that in mind, you should not be overly concerned about looking nervous. Instead, bring your chest forward, and stand upright as if you're wearing a crown.

Your face conveys trust, likeability, and competence. Whenever it's appropriate, share your passion and enthusiasm for your message.

Smile and mean it. Feel it in your entire body, heart and soul. If in doubt, picture a happy, smiling, chubby baby. A great smile can immediately engage and draw in your audience. But it's a good idea to match your audience's energy level at the beginning. Be mindful of plastering on a "permasmile." While appropriate for a model or dancer, a permanent smile on a presenter is the facial equivalent of speaking in monotone.

Eye contact

They say that the eyes are the window to the soul. At least in North America, effective eye contact signals confidence, competency, and trust. How purposeful is your eye contact during your presentation? What message do you convey?

Observe the audience in a slow, controlled fashion. If your eyes repeatedly dart left, right, up, and down when you speak, you won't look credible. If you don't look at your audience, they might wonder who you're speaking to. You'll seem hesitant, unsure, and untrustworthy. And if you speak while staring up at the ceiling or down at your notes, it's a challenge to create and maintain an emotional connection with your audience. Whether someone is confused, supportive, or playing *Candy Crush*, you must first see them before you can engage them.

Look for a few friendly faces in your audience that your eyes can always return to. You will often have conversational eye contact if you focus on one person at a time while you complete a thought. But make everyone feel included. Connect the best you can with those in the front, in the middle, and in the back of the audience, as well as those who may be seated along the side. Make your speech feel like more of a conversation, where you look at Tom, then at Dick, then at Harriet, rather than a theatrical monologue.

Hand gestures

You create pictures in the minds of your audience through your arm and hand gestures. What image do you want to illustrate for them?

For visual interest, avoid complete paralysis when presenting. To keep your delivery fresh, avoid compulsively repeating the same arm and hand gestures. Practice a variety of relevant movements and learn to use appropriate gestures you have mastered.

Open-palm gestures give an inviting, sincere, and heart

felt impression. Be careful with closed-palm gestures, such as a fist or pointing a finger at your audience. Such gestures can leave a condescending, aggressive, or accusatory impression.

Your gestures should support your words, timing, and emotion. Consider choreographing and rehearsing your hand movements in advance. Make sure they are relevant, and are neither distracting nor redundant.

Be aware that certain gestures have different meanings in other cultures. Giving your audience a thumbs up is a positive sign in many English-speaking countries. But it can be considered offensive in Thailand, Iran, and Afghanistan. Also, forming an "OK" sign with your thumb and index finger is acceptable in North America. But it's considered a rude gesture in countries such as Brazil, Germany, and Turkey.[26]

Footwork

Do you step with intention? Some speakers like to move, while others remain in one place. Either way, make your movement purposeful. Consider planting your feet firmly on the platform, like a tree. This stance conveys poise, authority, and confidence. As you transition to a new point in your presentation, consider stepping to the left or right. To emphasize an important point, step forward.

---

[26] Read more at http://j.mp/rude-gestures

Whenever you move, do so with purpose. Some speakers pace; this can lull the audience or convey an impression of nervous energy. Erratic movements distract and detract from your message. Move with purpose, to bring polish to your passion.

> *What you do speaks so loud that*
> *I cannot hear what you say.*

- RALPH WALDO EMERSON

 Activity

(1) Reflect on five key words in your presentation outline and think about gestures that reinforce the meaning of each word.

(2) On a scale of 1 to 10, rate your posture when speaking.

(3) On a scale of 1 to 10, how engaging is your eye contact with audience members?

(4) On a scale of 1 to 10, how aligned are your hand gestures with your message?

(5) Thank back to past presentations that you've given. What were some signs that you connected with your audience through your body language? What were some signs that you didn't?

Chapter 15
Involve Your Audience

Information is giving out;
communication is getting through.

- SYDNEY J. HARRIS

What can you offer your audience that they can't get from watching a video on YouTube?

You can allow them to participate in a customized and shared experience. Both you and your audience benefit from the mutual collaboration of a live, in-person event. Ask thoughtful questions to stimulate their thinking and to get them involved. As comedian John Oliver said, "I'm always interested in audience interaction. I'm genuinely interested in how people see things."

Remember to end on your own closing remarks, not on Q&A. Give yourself the last word. For details, refer to **Chapter 8: End with Excellence.**

Ask questions

When preparing beforehand, think carefully about how to phrase your questions. Is there any chance your queries could be misunderstood? Use clear, unambiguous language, and ensure that each request is appropriate for your audience.

When asking open or closed questions, at first no one may answer. Pause for a few seconds to let your audience gather their thoughts. When you see body language or visual cues that show someone has an idea, call on that person to reply.

Run through possible answers beforehand, so that you can advance the conversation regardless of the response.

Your questions can provoke thought, elicit a response, and allow you to assess their understanding. But questions must be meaningful to your audience and pertinent to the presentation.

Open-ended questions

Start and continue the conversation with open-ended questions. Open-ended questions elicit more detailed answers than a simple one- or two-word response.

For example: "What's the biggest challenge that you'd like to address today?"

Ask thought-provoking questions, but stay within the audience's realm of knowledge and experience.

Closed-ended questions

Use closed-ended questions to reinforce a point, confirm understanding, or end the discussion.

You may choose to elaborate after the answer, though. For instance: "Do you have any questions about *vocal fry*? The reason why I ask is because it's quite interest*eeeaaannng...*"

After asking a closed question you may receive both correct and incorrect answers. If the response is correct, acknowledge the participant's answer by repeating and reinforcing it. If the reply is incorrect, avoid embarrassing the responder. Instead, rephrase the question or call on someone else.

Rhetorical questions

Rhetorical questions provoke your audience. You may incite them to reflect on the past, picture the future, or challenge their biases. For example:

- "Have you ever found it hard to speak off the top of your head?"
- "How would Warren Buffett describe your presentation?"
- "What would you attempt if you knew you couldn't fail?

Use rhetorical questions to introduce a story, lead into an important point, or reinforce a message. They also make an excellent transition between topics.

There are usually no right or wrong responses. Rhetorical questions may not even have an answer. But provide enough time for your audience to silently reflect on your words. Pause, answer the question in your mind, and then continue.

Handle hecklers

If you address the audience's needs and interests, then you shouldn't have a problem with difficult behavior. This is especially true if your audience participates.

But not all audience members may be receptive to your efforts. Some may take you off-track during Q&A. To get back on track, highlight the current topic, restate the purpose, and remind the audience how they'll benefit.

What if a participant argues with you?

Stay calm. Acknowledge them and allow them to speak their mind. Paraphrase their issue, reflecting the meaning and feeling you heard from them. If necessary, ask probing questions to get to the underlying issue. As a last resort, suggest you continue the discussion after your presentation—then break eye contact and continue on.

What if a participant asks a long-winded question and monopolizes the conversation?

You have a responsibility to the other participants to handle the situation firmly and take back control. Answer the participant's question briefly. Then end the discussion by asking them a closed question to which they can only reply "yes" or "no." Or end the discussion by making a flat statement, and transitioning back to your topic.

Even with new technologies, it's a treat to be part of a live, shared, in-person experience. Ask thoughtful questions to make your audience's time more memorable.

Get standing ovations

Typically, there are three reasons why audiences give speakers a standing ovation.

Honored

At the 44th Academy Awards in 1972, actor Charlie Chaplin received a 12-minute standing ovation. He earned an honorary Oscar for "the incalculable effect he has had in making motion pictures the art form of this century." For his monumental contributions to the film industry, Charlie Chaplin received the longest standing ovation in the history of the Academy Awards. Are you being recognized for colossal accomplishments in your field?[27]

---

[27] See the video at http://j.mp/charlie-chaplin-speech

Wowed

As a result of the drug thalidomide, Hall of Fame professional speaker Alvin Law was born with no arms. But he learned to use his feet for hands. Despite having no arms, Alvin has accomplished what many "normal" people have only dreamed of. He became a professional speaker, award-winning musician, and bestselling author. He has been the subject of two award-winning documentaries, has spoken to over 7,500 organizations on five continents, and has helped raise nearly $200 million for charity.

We all face obstacles in our lives. But if a man without arms can accomplish so much with his life, what excuse do we have? Alvin sends a message of hope that any struggle in our own lives can be overcome. His life story is an inspiration and his show is enormously entertaining. Wouldn't you give Alvin a standing ovation, too?[28]

Invited

When professional coach and facilitator Maria Racelis was 24 years old, she had an epiphany while working in the insurance industry. Based on her outstanding first year in sales, Maria was invited to speak at her company's fall conference in front of one thousand

---

[28] See more at http://j.mp/alvinlaw

insurance agents.

After sharing her success story to the enthusiastic crowd, Maria wanted to conclude with impact. She decided to leave the audience with a positive affirmation they could use to jump start their day every morning. Taking a page from motivational speaker Zig Ziglar, Maria instructed the audience to: "Jump up off your seats!"

She declared, "Clap your hands!" and, "It's going to be a great day today!"

The audience followed her exact instructions, and they remained standing while Maria walked off the stage.

The emcee declared: "Now *that*, my friends, is how you get a standing ovation!"

 **Activity**

(1) Create an appropriate open and closed question for your presentation. Plan when you will use it.

(2) Craft an effective rhetorical question for your presentation. When will you use it? Will you repeat it, to reiterate a theme or reinforce a conclusion?

(3) How will you handle a situation where no one answers a question?

(4) Imagine a long-winded or hostile comment during Q&A. What will you say to get the session back on track?

(5) When was the last time you were in an audience that gave a standing ovation? How will it feel when you receive yours?

Your 7-Day Presentation Challenge

Want to create your next talk by next week? This *7-Day Presentation Challenge* will propel you into action—step by step and day by day.

Visit **rhtsang.com/book** to download your free *Fast Start Kit*, complete with the exercises, daily checklists, tracking sheets, and everything else you need to make starting the *7-Day Presentation Challenge* as easy as possible.

Find one or more people to be your accountability partner(s), and invite them to join you for the *7-Day Presentation Challenge*. Having someone else on your side increases your commitment to success and makes the journey even more fun!

Visit **rhtsang.com/book** to get started.

Epilogue

The major value in life is not what you get.
The major value in life is what you become.

- JIM ROHN

Are some people natural born speakers?

I wasn't. I was once a habitual mumbler, and even my own parents couldn't understand me! So I chose to become a serious student of speaking, and this book distills all my lessons learned along the way.

If I can do it, how about you?

You have expertise that's too important to keep to yourself. You have a story that needs to be shared. Always remember: your message is more important than you know!

To your standing ovation,

Ron

rhtsang.com/book

Join
Ovation Nation

Fans and readers of *From Presentation to Standing Ovation* have a free online community to connect, share best practises, discuss the book, get encouragement, and find accountability partners.

Collaborate with like-minded people to receive additional support and accelerate your growth. And you'll find me participating regularly in *Ovation Nation.*

Just go to **http://j.mp/ovationnation** and request to join *Ovation Nation* on Facebook. I look forward to seeing you there!

Acknowledgements

Thank you to my good friend Maria Racelis for pushing me outside my comfort zone, and for being there to celebrate all the milestones.

Thanks to Ameer Rosic and James Tonn for inspiring me to write this book, and for all your incredible ideas, feedback, and support along the way.

Thank you to Andrew Scopick for the great book title.

This work was made possible with the encouragement, feedback, and guidance of Carol Martin, Darrell Cheung, Dr. Natasha Vani, Nicky Billou, Michael Palmer, and Michael Santonato. Thank you.

Thank you to my editor, Victoria Barclay—the Text Medic—and my Stewardly proofreader, Josh Leslie.

Thanks for the extra book pizzazz Alvin Law, Anthony McLean, Dave Lieber, David Newman, Hal Elrod, Jayson Gaignard, Jon Goodman, Kaye Parker, Nina Spencer, and Tahani Aburaneh.

Thanks to my CAPS and NSA peeps for being friends and mentors, especially Beverly Beuerman-King, Carol Schulte, Donald Cooper, Gail Scott, Jana Stanfield, JJ

Brun, Kathryn McKenzie, Laurie Flasko, Lisa Latorcai, Michael Flint, Orlando Bowen, Patti Pokorchuk, Randall Craig, Renee Paser-Paull, Rose Adams, Ross Mackay, Sarah McVanel-Viney, Stephanie Staples, Steve Lowell, Sunjay Nath, Tom Stoyan, and Toni Newman.

Thank you to these very inspiring Toastmasters: Anna Taylor, Bala Iyengar, Blake Kurisko, Carmelita Dela Cruz, Deborah Austin, Dolores Pian, Elaine Lee, Elton Brown, Hondy Hung, Ileana Spilca, Janice Howard, Jim Kokocki, Julia Katsivo, Kathleen Wong, Kazuko Kawauchi, Kendra Shimmin, Kenneth Cheung, Lydia Chang, Marigrace King, Melanie Wijeratna, Myqeel Gayi, Peter Michaels, Phil Tasci, Rhonda Mauer, Tony Nelson, Ven Virah, and Wendy Williamson.

Thank you for fueling my growth, especially Alexandra DeSousa, Aunt Mo-Chi, Fady Sbeih, Floyd Marinescu, Giovanni Marsico, Kevin Leung, Jon Morrow, Lester Lau, Linda Yao, Lisette Andreyko, Marta Nowinska, Nicholas Kusmich, Patrick Scopick, Ramy Elitzur, Ron Grebler, Scott Oldford, Sidd Mehta, Sol Orwell, Stephen Clarke, Svetlana Ratnikova, and UJ Ramdas.

Special thanks: Adam Grant, Amy Cuddy, Brian Tracy, Craig Valentine, Darren LaCroix, Jack Canfield, Judy Carter, Mark Bowden, Nicholas Boothman, Patricia Fripp, Tony Robbins, and Warren Buffett.

Thank you to my incredible clients. Keep levelling up.

Thank YOU for reading—I appreciate you.

About the Author

RON TSANG specializes in working with professionals who want to deliver more successful presentations.

A former stock analyst, Ron has evaluated thousands of presentations from CEOs and CFOs. He knows what it takes to deliver unforgettable messages.

Ron is an in-demand speaker based in Toronto, Canada. He teaches business communication at The Business School at Centennial College and the University of Toronto's Rotman Executive Programs. He has also mentored senior managers at some of the world's largest financial institutions, manufacturing companies, and government agencies on presenting with power.

Ron has an MBA from the Rotman School of Management at the University of Toronto, and an HBA from the University of Waterloo.

Ron is on a mission to help one million experts achieve massive influence from speaking.

FREE speaking resources, templates, and tools are waiting for you online at **rhtsang.com/book**.

Praise for Ron's Seminars

"Ron is an inspiring speaker and teacher—full of energy and passion, he kept us engaged and entertained throughout the entire workshop."
  –Lydia Chang, Corporate Finance Manager, Nestlé

"His practical tips can dramatically improve your presentation immediately."
  –Kenneth Cheung, Director, BMO Financial Group

"The influence and guidance of Ron Tsang working with the groups was obvious."
  –Ron G. Bain, Executive Director,
  Ontario Association of Chiefs of Police

"Ron, you possess a special gift to bring out the best in others."
  –Darrell Cheung, Owner, Satori Health and Wellness

"I can't get enough of your awesome oratory skills, Ron! You could do a talk about the weather and I'd be on the edge of my seat!"
  –Floyd Marinescu, CEO, C4Media

Find out if Ron is available for your
next conference or in-house event.
Email info@rhtsang.com or call (647) 885-0227.

RON TSANG

FROM PRESENTATION
TO STANDING
OVATION

Get **free** companion tools and downloads at
rhtsang.com/book

Made in the USA
Monee, IL
04 March 2020

FROM PRESENTATION
TO STANDING
OVATION

"This extraordinary book is loaded with great ideas you can use immediately to become a more powerful and persuasive speaker."

–Brian Tracy, has given 5,000 speeches in 75 countri

"I'm glad Ron wrote this book because I'm a firm believer that the wisest investment is wisdom, and this book is full of wisdom."

–Jayson Gaignard, founder of MastermindTal

"If you need to quickly gain more confidence in captivating your audience every time you speak, then this book will really help!"

–Mark Bowden, TRUTHPLANE* Presentation Traini

"Ron Tsang has written THE definitive book on presenting with power, influence, and poise. Buy a copy for everyone on your team. Yes, it's that good."

–David Newman, CSP (Certified Speaking Professional) a
bestselling author of Do It! Marketi

"Ron has written a powerful tool for people to guide them to the highest level of presentations. Whether internal to small groups or external to thousands, the practical and philosophical information i this book is truly priceless!"

–Alvin Law, CSP (Certified Speaking Professional) a
Hall of Fame Speak

"Clear. Clever. Classy and Current. Ron Tsang gets my standing ovation. He has totally nailed it. My advice? Buy two copies and kee one locked up: this book has legs."

–Nicholas Boothman, bestselling author
How to Make People Like You In 90 Seconds Or Le

RON TSANG can help **you**—the way he helps experts at some of the world's largest banks, manufacturing companies, and government agencies deliver captivating keynotes, close important deals, and achieve massive influence.

For free templates, resources and downloads, visit
rhtsang.com/book

ISBN 9781517455989

90000

9 781517 455989

Photo by Ron Grebler
Cover design by Fady Sbeih

Captain P.I. Rikord's Voyages to Japan during 1811-1813

Bicentennial Anniversary Edition
Commemorating the Release of His Comrades from Captivity

『国立公文書館所蔵』
Japanese National Archives

麟勝堂

Lin Sho Doh